AF521168

Why My Horse Doesn't Drink

Why My Horse Doesn't Drink

VIVEK MEHROTRA

Viva Books

New Delhi | Mumbai | Chennai | Kolkata | Bengaluru | Hyderabad | Kochi | Guwahati

Publisher's Notes

Every possible effort has been made to ensure that the information contained in this book is accurate at the time of going to press, and the publishers and authors cannot accept responsibility for any errors or omissions, however caused. No responsibility for loss or damage occasioned to any person acting, or refraining from action, as a result of the material in this publication can be accepted by the editor, the publisher or any of the authors.

Every effort has been made to trace the owner of copyright material used in this book. The author and the publisher will be grateful for any omission brought to their notice for acknowledgement in the future edition of this book.

Copyright © Viva Books Private Limited, 2005

First Published 2005
Reprinted 2006, 2009, 2012

VIVA BOOKS PRIVATE LIMITED

- 4737/23 Ansari Road, Daryaganj, New Delhi 110 002
  E-mail: vivadelhi@vivagroupindia.net, Tel. 42242200
- 76, Service Industries, Shirvane, Sector 1, Nerul, Navi Mumbai 400 706
  E-mail: vivamumbai@vivagroupindia.net, Tel. 27721273, 27721274
- Jamals Fazal Chambers, 26 Greams Road, Chennai 600 006
  E-mail: vivachennai@vivagroupindia.net, Tel. 28290304, 28294241
- B-103, Jindal Towers, 21/1A/3 Darga Road, Kolkata 700 017
  E-mail: vivakolkata@vivagroupindia.net, Tel. 22836381, 22816713
- 7, Sovereign Park Apartments, 56-58, K. R. Road, Basavanagudi, Bengaluru 560 004
  E-mail: vivabangalore@vivagroupindia.net, Tel. 26607409, 26607410
- 101-102 Mughal Marc Apartments, 3-4-637 to 641, Narayanguda, Hyderabad 500 029
  E-mail: vivahyderabad@vivagroupindia.net, Tel. 27564481, 27564482
- First Floor, Beevi Towers, SRM Road, Kaloor, Kochi 682 018, Kerala
  E-mail: vivakochi@vivagroupindia.net, Tel: 0484-2403055, 2403056
- 232, GNB Road, Beside UCO Bank, Silpukhuri, Guwahati 781 003
  E-mail: vivaguwahati@vivagroupindia.net, Tel: 0361-2666386

www.vivagroupindia.com

All rights reserved. No part of this book may be reproduced or utilized in any form or by any means, electronic or mechanical, including photocopying, recording or by any information storage or retrieval systems, without permission in writing from the publisher.

ISBN : 978-81-309-0096-4

Published by Vinod Vasishtha for Viva Books Private Limited, 4737/23, Ansari Road, Daryaganj, New Delhi - 110 002. Printed and bound by Sanat printers, Kundli - 131 028, Haryana.

Dedicated to
All
Practising Managers

Foreword

"You can take a horse to the pond but cannot make it drink" is an old proverb. However, the irony is that it is true of human beings as well. Have you ever wondered:

- "Why doesn't this person work?"
- "Why doesn't this person work on this project/assignment?"
- "Why do I always get bad people (colleagues and superiors) to work with?"
- "Could someone be more ungrateful than this person?"
- "Why does this colleague hate me?"
- "Why does this person want to embarrass me?"

If yes, go on reading this book. You will be able to explore:

- Why some people behave in a particular fashion.
- What makes people work and produce extraordinary results.
- Why some people refuse to work even when they are paid better than others.
- What makes people dissatisfied at the workplace.
- Why some people don't get along with others.

Apart from answering the above questions, this book will help you understand basic human needs, which keep driving a person towards the goal one has set for oneself. This book will also answer the question why some people are highly motivated whereas others are not.

Eventually the book will help you increase the productivity of your team members by improving their job satisfaction.

S. Sreenivas Rao
Prof. (Retd.)
Indian Institute of Management
Ahmedabad

Preface

The words of the British Prime Minister Sir Winston Churchill spoken during the World War II, embody the essence of this book: "This is not the end. It is not even the beginning of the end. It may possibly be the end of the beginning." No book on the subject 'Motivation' would probably cover the subject fully and for all times. I have tried to describe motivation in an all-encompassing perspective. This does not mean that every aspect of the subject has been covered. That would be impossible. Because Motivation is highly intrinsic and individualized; readers themselves will need to understand what motivates an individual team member and accordingly may work upon it.

Majority of the books on Motivation are written from the point of view of an employer. Most of the issues are discussed in terms of employer–employee relationships. However, a practising manager has a very limited role as far as job content, design or working conditions are concerned. Nevertheless, he has an important role to play, i.e. creating the right environment for people to feel motivated and perform. Although almost all the books on motivation emphasize the need for creating the right environment, how to do so remains unanswered. This book will help readers create a conducive and congenial work environment.

Another important role a practising manager needs to play effectively is to carry out performance appraisal and provide feedback to his team members on a regular basis. Though all of us know recognition and reward motivate a person, on many occasions we fail to do so. This book will help readers understand the concept "Things that get rewarded get done." A manager who fails to reward right behaviour gets the wrong results.

This book will serve as an introduction to the various concepts associated with Motivation and will enable the readers to put all the specifics into a coherent framework. If a practising manager wants to influence the people around him both on a personal and professional level, there is no other way than through understanding their needs.

Motivation is like an accelerator in a vehicle. A vehicle keeps moving at the pace decided by its accelerator. The moment the accelerator is reduced, the vehicle's speed reduces and it may come to a standstill if there is no further acceleration. Alternatively, if brakes are applied, there will be an abrupt reduction in the speed of the vehicle and it may come to a standstill.

This is true to human beings as well. As long as they are motivated they keep working and producing extraordinary results. The moment there is a drop in their acceleration (motivation), results start diminishing. Of course, applying brakes (dissatisfaction/demotivation) certainly brings them to a halt. The only difference is that unlike a vehicle, human beings have different types of accelerators and brakes.

This book will help readers identify the factors that may accelerate or slow down the speed of their team members. The chapter 'How to Motivate' talks about the points that accelerate and the chapter 'How Not to Demotivate' explains the factors that may work as brakes to the performance. Thereby readers will be able to make the best use of their vehicle (team members).

It would be of great help if readers could share their comments, advice, criticism or suggestions at vivekmehrotra@rediffmail.com. Any real-life story of direct or indirect motivation or demotivation, before or after applying ideas and material from the book, is welcome. This feedback will help me to improve the future editions.

VIVEK MEHROTRA

Acknowledgment

"Bad poets borrow;" however, "good poets steal," T.S. Eliot said. Jack Welch, CEO of GE, coined another phrase "Steal shamelessly." Nevertheless, the key message remains the same. There is no harm in taking a clue from anywhere in the world, as long as one can further elaborate on the same idea. In fact it helps everyone, as many others get to know about the great idea.

I am not Abhimanyu, who knew the art of breaking the *chakravyuh* even before he was born. While writing this book it was my earnest endeavour to adopt (steal) ideas and concepts related to motivation from all the possible sources. What I did was to first absorb the idea, its importance and relationship to the relevant chapter, and then rework it to suit the topic. I have taken help right from our ancient scriptures to the latest articles and books published on the subject, 'Motivation'. Unfortunately, sources were not always noted or available; hence, it is not possible for me to mention the name of each and everyone whose ideas I have used in my book. Through this paragraph it is my heartfelt attempt to acknowledge their hidden contribution to the book.

I would like to thank Viva Books for support and believing in my book. I am also thankful to my friends, colleagues and seniors for their patient listening to my ideas, reading the drafts and helping me to revise, modify or change it.

I will remain indebted to Prof. S. Sreenivas Rao, Prof. Pramod Verma of Indian Institute of Management, Ahmedabad and Ms. Nivedita Kothiyal for their invaluable contribution to the book.

At the end, let me express gratitude to my parents and family members for my upbringing. Last but not the least, I acknowledge the support of my wife, without whose support it would not have been possible for me to complete this book.

Acknowledgement

How to Make Best Use of This Book?

At the outset let me narrate a story.

'EAT YOUR OWN FRUIT'

Some disciples one day asked their guru, "Guruji, you tell us stories but never tell us their meaning."

The Guru replied, "How would you feel if someone offers you a fruit after chewing it?"

The moral of the story is that nobody can teach or train anybody. It is the individual who puts the learning into practice and thus trains himself. Hence, experiential learning is the best form of learning, as it lasts much longer.

You would benefit to the extent you are willing to practise the learning from the book and apply it to everyday issues and challenges. Therefore, you must not hurry in finishing the book. Instead you must relate the examples given in this book with your own experiences. Specially, while reading through the chapter 'How Not to Demotivate'. You must ponder on each reason mentioned as a cause of dissatisfaction. You should ask yourself, "Am I creating any such situation for my team members?" If your answer is "yes", you should immediately write down those situations. In future, while dealing with your team members you must take due precautions and avoid any such situation that may dissatisfy or demotivate your team member. Both 'Tips' and the 'Word of Caution' given in this book will help you to chalk out a remedial course of action.

Your success will depend solely upon your ability to identify and work upon an individual's motivators, and at the same time by refraining from creating demotivators.

You will notice that throughout this book I have used masculine gender while addressing an individual. It is done for the ease of writing and not out of gender bias. The concepts mentioned in this book remain common for both the genders.

VIVEK MEHROTRA

Contents

Introduction

MOTIVATION

The word 'motivation' is among the six most-used words in any company's documents. Although motivation is a widely talked-about topic, it is the least understood subject. It is the most powerful tool for getting things done from human beings.

MOTIVATION: EQUATION

P = F (M, A, E)

P: *Performance*
is a
F: *Function*
of
M: *Motivation*
A: *Ability*
and
E: *Environment*

The performance of your team members is an outcome of motivation, ability and above all the environment he gets both at the workplace and at home. Most of the managers focus their efforts on improving the ability of their team members. However, very little attention is paid to the individual's motivation and towards creating a conducive work environment. Since as a manager your success directly depends upon your team members' success, it is important for you to give equal importance and attention to all the three factors.

> **"There are two things that motivate a person to succeed: inspiration and desperation."**
>
> **— Anthony Robbins**

MOTIVATION: CASE STUDIES

CASE 1

In 1982, when the American airline industry was facing one of the worst recessions, 25,000 employees of an airline together raised a fund of $ 30 million. They bought their employer a new aircraft.

What motivated the employees to do this?

- Did they want to reciprocate the company's past gestures towards them?
- Did they have a feeling of ownership?
- Was it their loyalty towards the organization?
- Were they afraid that if the company went out of business they would lose their jobs?

CASE 2

A woman employee of a leading FMCG company worked in the factory. One day, while shopping in the local supermarket, she came across a shelf full of jars of peanut butter manufactured by her own factory. To her surprise, the labels of a few jars were upside down. She bought all those jars and took them to the factory with her the next day.

What motivated her to do that?

- Was it a matter of prestige for her to work for 'this' organization, and this type of packaging of products do not match with the same?
- Was it her loyalty towards the organization which made her buy all the defective pieces?
- Is it that she herself was working in the packaging department and was afraid of being penalized, in case her superior would see these jars?
- Was it that she wanted to bring the matter to the notice of her superiors to get a reward or to malign a colleague?

CASE 3

Rama, a 32-year-old lady who holds a degree in human resource, works as the personnel manager for Asia Garments, a small manufacturer of readymade garments. She earns Rs. 1,50,000 per year with no other perks.

However, she loves working at Asia; she often takes work home.

What makes Rama not only continue working at Asia Garments, but enjoy it too?

- Is it money?
- Is it that she gets satisfaction due to flexibility and autonomy of work at Asia?
- Is it that nobody at Asia supervises closely the activities of employees?
- Is it that the employees at Asia are free to take decisions about their job?

What makes different people do what they do?

Can you pinpoint the reason(s) and say confidently that because of this particular reason, every employee of the airline contributed to the corpus of fund? There might have been hundreds of reasons for which different employees contributed. However, the fact remains that everybody contributed.

The reason the woman employee brought the defective bottles back to her workplace could be any one of the above mentioned reasons, or may be something else.

Similarly, is it the money that kept Rama motivated to work extra hours without any extra compensation?

There are different reasons for different people for the same act.

Have you ever tried to find out the reason that keeps each team member, including you, on his toes and is responsible for bringing the best out of everyone? It is the individual's motivation that propels him to do extraordinary acts. Nevertheless, the level of motivation varies between individuals and within individuals at different times.

Several myths are associated with the word 'motivation'. Therefore, before we discuss the ways to get a person motivated, let us examine some popular myths about motivation.

MOTIVATION: SOME MYTHS

MYTH 1: MONEY IS ALWAYS AN EFFECTIVE MOTIVATOR

No, it is not. No doubt, everyone wants money; but it is not the only reason that makes people perform extraordinary tasks. In fact, it is observed that people keep working for a company for money but do not necessarily produce extraordinary results. On the contrary, people take initiative and produce extraordinary results because of their own motivation. Take the example of the woman employee of the FMCG company. In fact, money and job satisfaction are two wings of a bird; one is enough for survival, but to fly high both are required.

Money and job satisfaction are the two wings of a bird. One is enough for survival, but to fly high both are required.

MYTH 2: MANAGERS CAN MOTIVATE

Managers propagate the myth that they can easily motivate a person. By the time you have read this book you will realize how difficult it is to motivate somebody. On the other hand, it is very easy to demotivate. Nobody can motivate anybody. Motivation is an inner feeling, a desire, an inclination that compels a person to act or behave in a certain manner.

An individual gets motivated or demotivated solely because of himself. Therefore, what best a manager, or anybody, can do is to create the environment which keeps a person motivated.

MYTH 3: MOTIVATORS ARE UNIVERSAL

Most of us commit the mistake of handling all our team members in the same manner. We forget that what motivates one does not necessarily motivate the other. Different people have different needs. It is their craving for fulfilling these needs that pushes them to put in extra effort. For instance, a person in the early years of his career may be more concerned about money. However, over a period, job security matters more to him than money. On the contrary, a senior team member may not be as disappointed on not getting an incentive as on missing a promotion. Similarly, an older employee instead of promotion will opt for stability. Remember, each person's motivation is different; hence you need "different strokes for different folks".

> **"Different people are capable of different levels of success. However, most underestimate their capabilities."**
>
> **— Unknown**

MYTH 4: ONCE MOTIVATED, ALWAYS MOTIVATED

You must have observed that after the annual conference or annual day function of a company, the team members get really charged. In other words, they get motivated to do whatever is asked for, even if it is a Herculean task. However, as soon as they return to their office/territories, their enthusiasm evaporates. It is like blowing a balloon. If you do not tie a knot, the air will go out. Remember, motivation is not a one-time booster; it is an on-going process.

> **"Motivation is like food for the brain. You cannot get enough in one sitting. It needs continual and regular top-ups".**
>
> **— Peter Davies**

MOTIVATION: AN EXPLANATION

According to one hypothesis, the word 'motivation' comes from the Latin word 'movere', meaning to set in motion. No movement takes place in a person until his motivation forces him to do so. A person remains in a state of inertia until he is motivated to do an act.

Physics and human nature have many similarities. You must be aware of Newton's laws of motion and their applications. However, do you know that these laws apply to human nature as accurately as they apply to physics?

> **"Motivation is the fuel necessary to keep the human engine running."**
>
> **— Zig Ziglar**

Newton's First Law of *Motivation* (Motion)

Every body persists in its state of rest or uniform motion in a straight line unless compelled to change that state by force impressed on it.

According to Newton's First Law of Motion, an object remains in a state of inertia or in uniform motion until an external agency makes it change its state. This external agency is known as force. Similarly, human beings do not change their state of affairs unless a force is applied on them. People do not take initiative or an action until they are compelled to do so. This force could be external, i.e., due to the influence of others, such as friends, parents, teachers, peers and superiors. However, ultimately this force is internalized as whether to be influenced or not depends upon the individual's own will. This force is motivation.

> **"Motivation is the force that causes people to act or behave differently."**
>
> **— Unknown**

Another explanation about the origin of the word 'motivation' is that it comes from the word 'motive'. According to this hypothesis, there is always a motive behind every act of a person. Without a motive, a person does not act.

The premise of 'Court of Justice' is based upon finding out the motive behind the crime. According to law, the origin of the word 'crime' is from two Latin words 'mens rea', i.e. the 'guilty mind', without which any action remains an 'act' and not an 'offence.' According to the Indian Penal Code, section 302, a person is not to be penalized by death or life sentence for a murder committed in self-defence. However, a person may be penalized under section 307 to rigorous imprisonment of seven years for shooting somebody (not necessarily killing the person), 'if his motive was to kill him, i.e. an attempt to murder.

These descriptions of the word 'motivation' do not explain why people always act in a certain way or keep doing an act repetitively and why there is a difference in the responses of people to the same situations or stimuli. For example, in the same organization or team some people work harder than others do. Why does somebody put in extraordinary efforts towards a task while others do very little? To understand it, let us once again take the help of Newton's laws of motion.

Newton's Second Law of *Motivation* (Motion)

The rate of change of momentum of a body is proportional to the applied force and takes place in the direction in which the force acts.

According to this law, it is the applied force, which decides how long a moving mass will continue to move in a particular direction. Here 'force' is a resultant of mass and acceleration. What is acceleration? It is the rate of change of 'velocity'.

Since, the mass (individual's competence) remains constant, it is the person's desire/interest (the velocity) that decides the extent of his success. More the desire and interest towards a particular job, better is the chance of success.

> **"The mechanics of industry is easy. The real engine is the people, their motivation and direction."**
>
> **— Ken Gilbert**

MOTIVATION: WHAT IS IT?

Motivation is the willingness of an individual to exert high levels of effort towards organizational and individual goals or needs. This explains why people always act in a certain manner or keep doing an act repetitively.

Very often the words velocity and speed are used interchangeably. However, they are different. Velocity has both magnitude as well as direction, whereas speed has only magnitude. Therefore, if the actions of an individual are not aligned in the direction that helps to achieve his goals, he can gain speed but will not reach his destination. In other words, he will work hard and much faster than others, yet will not get the desired results. Therefore, it is your duty to set the direction for your team members, so that their motivation, 'the force', works as velocity and takes them to the heights of success.

Motivation is the willingness of an individual to exert high levels of effort towards organizational and individual goals or needs.

Motivated individuals display distinct behaviour patterns, which are labelled as motivated behaviour.

Desire (Determination)

A motivated individual has a strong desire to achieve and, therefore, directs all his efforts towards the accomplishment of the goal. For example, if an individual's motivation is to earn money, he may work either more and try to earn through overtime/incentive or may take up an assignment outside the organization. In other words, a motivated individual is always determined to succeed.

Strength (Dedication)

The response of a motivated individual is always stronger than that of a person who is not motivated. A motivated individual is always dedicated to the cause and, therefore, puts in his best. For example, the response of an individual who has to support a large family or a younger brother for studies will certainly be greater than that of the one who needs money for his own leisure.

Variability (Creativity)

The most important characteristic of motivated behaviour is the search for an alternative path to reach the goal. When a motivated individual encounters a block, physical or mental, he does not get frustrated, but tries to find an alternative path for reaching the goal. His creativity increases. Here creativity means the net psychological energy that propels him to act differently.

Body Language of a Motivated Person

Motivated persons reflect enthusiasm and speak about the future with hope and expectation. They are full of zest for life. Whatever they do is always with a purpose. One enjoys the company of these people. You can make out a motivated person by his very appearance.

- He looks smart and has an appealing personality.
- Right from clothes, hair and shoes, he cares for himself.
- He makes an immediate impression about who he is.
- The face always wears a smile, eyes sparkle, and facial expressions are positive.
- He is bubbling with enthusiasm.

Body Language of a Demotivated Person

Demotivated persons reflect lack of enthusiasm and speak about the past with hopelessness. They have no zest for life. One feels frustrated in their company. Just like a motivated person, even a demotivated person can be easily identified by his looks:

- He is careless about clothes, hair and shoes.
- His face communicates lack of interest in work or in people.
- He avoids looking at you directly. Even if he looks at you, his face is expressionless.
- The condition of his workplace/work bag or detailing folder is extremely poor.
- He walks as if he is dragging his body.

MOTIVATION: CHARACTERISTICS

We described motivation as the willingness to exert high levels of effort towards organizational goals and individual needs. What is the genesis of this force, which is labelled as motivation? There are three key elements in our explanation of motivation – effort, organizational or personal goals, and individual needs. Human behaviour is an outcome of these three factors. An individual's needs, goals and motivation are intricately tied together and account for different responses from the individual in different situations. Let us try to understand in detail these factors and their relationship with one another.

Need

A 'need' is an internal state of mind that makes certain outcomes appear attractive to an individual – something a person lacks and feels that he must have.

Biological Needs

Hunger, thirst, rest/sleep and sex. These are the needs that are common to all human beings.

Psychological Needs

This is the need to establish and maintain satisfactory relations with other people. These needs vary with individuals depending upon his need with respect to interaction and association, control and power, love and affection from other people.

Goal (Motive)

Goal is the end towards which an individual directs his efforts. When an individual has a particular need, his goal is to satisfy that need. Just like needs, motives too are of two types.

Biological Motives

Biological motives are based upon the social environment. These motives must have social approval. For example, you must have observed people of a particular community avoid taking certain food on certain days or take food only at a particular time. The reasons for these actions may be to satisfy their elders or to be recognized as a member of a particular caste or religion.

Psychological Motives

Psychological motives include joy, fear, hate, anger, love, etc. Joy and love are positive emotions, whereas fear, hate and anger are negative emotions. Due to these positive and negative emotions, the direction and strength of action or behaviour of an individual varies in different situations. A positive emotion brings positive results. A negative emotion brings either reduced or no results. Of course, there are times when even a negative emotion, such as fear, may bring positive results.

Motivation: Need Satisfaction

MOTIVATION: NEED SATISFACTION

As long as a particular need remains unsatisfied, it creates some kind of tension in the mind of an individual and stimulates or drives him towards fulfilling that particular need. This stimulation or drive generates a search for behaviour to achieve the goals (fulfilling the needs). Once the need is satisfied, there is a reduction in the tension. Once again, there is a reassessment of needs, and the individual will have a different need or set of needs. There is no end to it. This reassessment of needs continues all through our life! Hence, we can also consider motivation as a need satisfying process.

Motivation is the desire to satisfy the need to achieve set goals. Stronger the desire, greater the motivation.

Motivated employees are always in a state of tension. To relieve this tension, they exert extraordinary effort. Greater the tension, higher the effort. If the effort leads to the satisfaction of need, the tension is reduced.

A word of caution:

Unwarranted tension leads to stress, which is detrimental to both the individual's performance as well as his health.

POINTS TO REMEMBER

MOTIVATION: AN INTRODUCTION

- Motivation is an inner feeling, a desire, and an inclination that compels a person to act or behave in a certain manner.
- Different people have different needs; it is their craving for fulfilling these needs that pushes them to put in extraordinary efforts.
- The level of motivation varies among individuals and within individuals at different times.
- Nobody can motivate anybody. An individual gets motivated or demotivated solely because of himself. What best one can do is to create the environment which keeps a person motivated.
- No doubt, money is a necessity for survival of an individual, yet it is not always an effective motivator. In order to be successful and happy, apart from money, job satisfaction is equally important.
- Each person's motivation is different; hence one needs "different strokes for different folks".
- Motivation is just not a one-time booster; it is an on-going process.
- Motivation is the most powerful tool for getting things done from human beings.
- Human beings do not change their state of affairs until a force is applied on them. This force is motivation, the force that causes people to act or behave differently.
- Motivation is the willingness of an individual to exert high level of efforts towards organizational and individual goals or needs.
- An individual's needs, goals and motivation are intricately tied together and account for different responses from the individual in different situations.
- Motivation is the desire to satisfy the need to achieve set goals; stronger the desire, greater the motivation.
- Motivated employees are always in a state of tension. To relieve this tension, they exert extraordinary effort. Greater the tension, higher the effort; if the effort leads to the satisfaction of the need, the tension is reduced.
- Joy and love are positive emotions, whereas fear, hate and anger are negative emotions. Due to these positive and negative emotions, the direction and strength of action or behaviour of an individual varies in different situations.

Theories of Motivation

EARLY THEORIES OF MOTIVATION

Some of the early theories formulated to explain the concept of motivation are:

- Abraham Maslow's Hierarchy of Needs
- Douglas McGregor's X & Y Theory
- Frederick Herzberg's Motivation–Hygiene Theory

Although the validity of all these theories is questionable, they are the best-known explanations of motivation. These theories in fact represent a foundation on which many contemporary theories have been built.

Maslow's Hierarchy of Needs

Abraham Maslow, the American psychologist, for the first time tried to explain motivation. According to his hypothesis, every human being has five basic needs:

1. Physiological needs (hunger, thirst, shelter, sex, clothing)
2. Safety needs (security, protection from physical or emotional harm)
3. Social needs (love and affection, sense of belonging, acceptance by people, friendship)
4. Esteem needs (self-respect, autonomy, achievement; status, recognition, and attention)
5. Self-actualization (The drive to become what one is capable of becoming; achieving one's own potential, self-fulfilment)

According to Maslow, there is a hierarchy of needs within an individual, i.e., physiological, safety, social, esteem, and self-actualization. Maslow classified these needs into higher and lower levels.

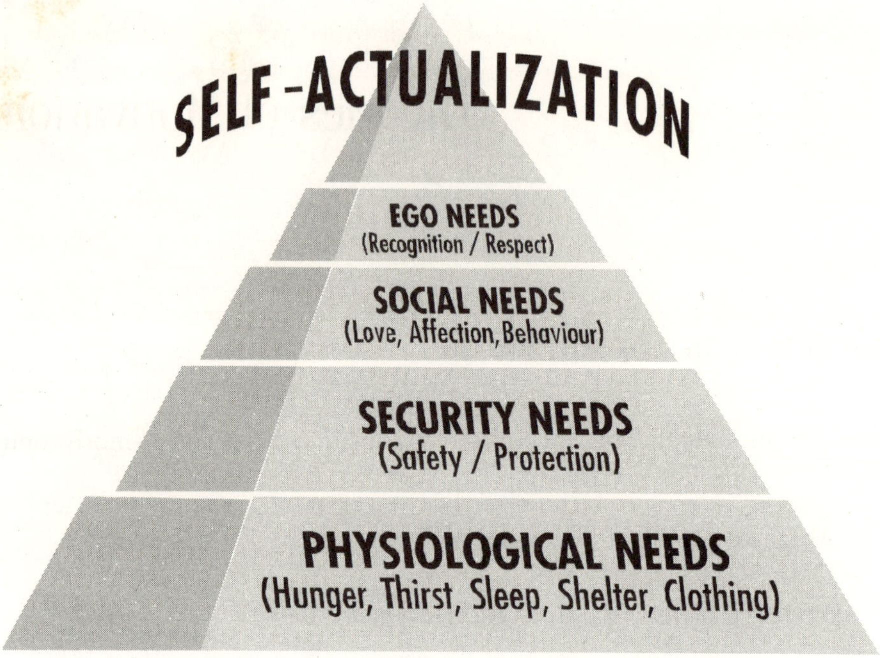

Motivational Pyramid

Lower order of needs: Needs satisfied externally (physiological and safety needs)

Higher order of needs: Needs satisfied internally (social needs, esteem, and self-actualization)

According to Maslow, once the lower order of needs gets substantially satisfied, an individual moves up the hierarchy and the next order of needs becomes predominant.

According to Maslow, although no need is ever fully gratified, a substantially satisfied need no longer motivates a person.

> **If you want to motivate someone, according to this theory, you need to understand where exactly that person currently is on the hierarchy and focus on satisfying the needs at or above that particular level.**

Maslow's theory was criticized the world over. It is debated whether all the needs in the hierarchy are always present in every person or they vary from person to person. Is it true that unsatisfied needs always motivate a person, or a satisfied need activates an individual towards a new need level? However, this theory is very popular, particularly among practising managers because it is based on an intuitive logic and is easy to understand and relate to.

> **"A musician must make music, an artist must paint, a poet must write, if he is to be ultimately happy. What a man can be, he must be. This is self-actualization."**
>
> **— Maslow**

Theory X and Theory Y

Douglas McGregor in his book *Human Side of Enterprise* pointed out how human beings develop different viewpoints towards their counterparts while interacting with them. He particularly studied the interactions between managers and subordinates. He highlighted two distinct views of managers towards their subordinates: one negative, which he labelled as Theory X, and the other positive, or Theory Y.

Theory X

According to Theory X, human beings in general dislike work, are lazy and do not like to shoulder responsibility, and unless forced to perform, they do not work.

This theory highlights the negative assumptions of managers about their subordinates, such as:

1. Human beings do not like to work and avoid it whenever possible.
2. Since people do not like to work, they must be forced/controlled/ threatened to achieve set goals.
3. Human beings do not like to shoulder responsibilities and try to avoid it whenever possible.
4. Most of the subordinates prefer to be managed instead of exercising self-control.
5. People in general have relatively little ambition; they give more importance to security than to other factors associated with work.

> **"People prefer to follow those who help them, not those who intimidate them."**
>
> **— C. Gene Wilkes**

Theory Y

Theory Y assumes that people like work, are creative, seek responsibility, and can exercise self-control. Under this theory McGregor listed positive assumptions of managers about their subordinates:

1. Work itself can be a source of satisfaction or dissatisfaction, depending upon certain controllable conditions.
2. External controls and punishment threats are not the only means of stimulating/directing efforts of human beings towards their goals.

3. People can exercise self-control and choose their direction provided they are committed to the objectives.
4. The average person can end up accepting and assuming responsibilities.
5. Imagination and creativity are not limited to a few selected ones holding management positions. Rather, these qualities can be found in anybody.

"To handle yourself, use your head; to handle others, use your heart."

— Donald Laird

Implications of McGregor's Theory

According to McGregor, managers, based on their assumption of their subordinates, categorize them either as falling in Theory X or Theory Y. In practice, however, no human being can be categorized into Theory X or Theory Y. In different situations human beings respond differently. McGregor himself preferred Theory Y.

If you are in sales, every day you are not with your team members. Moreover, you have to manage your team from a distant place. You may find it all the more important to adopt Theory Y to avoid unnecessary apprehension of your team members and disharmony.

Theory Z

Theory Z was developed by William Ouchi. In his book *Theory Z: How American Management Can Meet the Japanese Challenge,* Ouchi, a professor of management at UCLA, advocated a combination of all that is good about Theory Y and modern Japanese management that emphasizes on freedom to people. It also assumes that people have a strong loyalty towards the organization and interest in team-working.

Unlike McGregor's Theory X & Theory Y, that are focused on management and motivation from the manager's and organization's perspective, Theory Z places faith in the attitude and responsibilities of the people. Remember, the key to manage human beings lies in flexibility. Therefore, instead of following Theory X or Theory Y, you may adopt Theory Z, i.e., assess the situation, adapt to the individual's requirement and act accordingly.

Sometimes, due to a particular behaviour of your team member, you may develop negative opinion about him. In such situations, instead of reacting or adopting a threatening posture you must try to find out the reason for the indifferent behaviour. Most of the time, you will realize that the cause for the inconsistent behaviour is not the person himself but some external factors. If you can help remove the obstacle, you will not only win his confidence but will also be able to change his mindset.

Group participation in decision making, challenging jobs, and good interpersonal relations among team members maximize an individual's motivation towards his job.

Motivation–Hygiene Theory

Both Maslow's and McGregor's theories described the motivational concept in general. Frederick Herzberg's Motivation–Hygiene Theory explains motivational concept in the context of people working in the corporate sector. According to Herzberg, success or failure of an individual largely depends upon the person's attitude towards work/job. It is the satisfaction or dissatisfaction which one gets from the job that decides the individual's motivational levels. To prove his point Herzberg asked hundreds of accountants and engineers "what they wanted from their jobs". He asked them to describe in detail work situations when they felt exceptionally good and put extraordinary efforts to perform their job. Similarly, to describe situations when they felt bad about their jobs, which switched off their interest towards the job.

Factors leading to job satisfaction

Remember, money and job satisfaction are the two wings of a bird; one wing is enough for survival, but to fly high both wings are required. Herzberg's theory suggests that the opposite of satisfaction is not necessarily dissatisfaction. This means that the factors leading to job satisfaction are different and distinct from those that lead to job dissatisfaction. Hence, according to Herzberg, the opposite of 'satisfaction' is 'lack of satisfaction' and the opposite of 'dissatisfaction' is 'no dissatisfaction'. For example, it is observed that people, who are dissatisfied because of low pay, may change the company for getting higher pay. But does the higher pay in the new company necessarily make them satisfied and motivated? Higher pay may make them 'less dissatisfied' or 'not dissatisfied' as far as earning is concerned. However, if other factors, which satisfy people in general, are missing, will they necessarily be motivated?

Herzberg labelled the factors, which affect an individual's satisfaction/ dissatisfaction and ultimately job performance, as motivators and hygiene factors.

> **"In motivating people, you've got to engage their minds and their hearts."**
>
> **— Rupert Murdoch**

Motivators

These are the characteristics that people find intrinsically rewarding. Therefore, Herzberg suggests that to motivate people on their jobs, managers must emphasize these factors. The factors that Herzberg found consistently related to job satisfaction are:

1. Achievement

It is observed that the sense of achievement itself motivates a person. The classic example is of athletes. You must have heard of Sergi Bubka, who broke his own records in pole vault year after year.

2. Recognition/Reward

Recognition/reward further motivates a person to put extra effort in his job. It increases the person's self-esteem and creates a feeling of accomplishment.

> **"It is literally true that you can succeed best and quickest by helping others to succeed."**
>
> **— Napoleon Hill**

3. Work itself

Work is a constant source of motivation. A person is not tired because of the amount of workload but because of lack of interest in the job.

> **Recall a successful day, when you never felt tired or upset, although you worked for long hours. But on the day you failed in a few initial tasks, you must have felt tired. Have you ever tried to analyse the reason for your tirelessness or tiredness?**

4. Responsibility

If a person is given responsibility, he tries to discharge it in the best possible manner. The person considers the responsibility as a reward and tries to put extra effort to prove that he is suitable for holding such responsibility. On the contrary, if the person considers the responsibility a burden, he gets demotivated and stops putting in even the usual effort.

5. Advancement/Growth

Growth is a necessity of life. Right from birth, growth is the basic instinct of human beings, which stimulates their overall development. If your team members find their job as a source of growth in their competencies, they will feel motivated. Hence, it is your responsibility to help your team members develop their competencies, which will ultimately lead them to achieve their career goals.

> **"A feeling of continuous growth is a wonderful source of motivation and self-confidence."**
>
> **— Brian Tracey**

Hygiene Factors

Dissatisfaction among the people may be due to company policy and administration, close supervision, interpersonal relations, and working conditions. Herzberg labelled these factors as hygiene factors. When these factors are present in a job, they calm down the employees and make them feel there is no dissatisfaction or less dissatisfaction.

> **If you can eliminate factors that create job dissatisfaction, you can bring about peace. This, however, will not necessarily motivate your team members.**

Herzberg's theory confirms that people value factors like achievement, recognition and challenging work more than things like pay or security.

Although Herzberg's theory appears to be more accurate especially for the workforce in general and managers in particular, it has been highly criticized.

> **"A good objective of leadership is to help those who are doing poorly to do well and to help those who are doing well to do even better."**
>
> **— Jim Rohn**

POINTS TO REMEMBER

THEORIES OF MOTIVATION

- According to Maslow, although no need ever fully gratified, a substantially satisfied need no longer motivates the person.
- According to McGregor, managers, based on their assumption of their subordinates, categorize them either as falling in Theory X or Theory Y. In practice, however, no human being can be categorized into Theory X or Theory Y. In different situations, human beings respond differently.
- Flexibility is the key to handling human beings. One has to adapt to the individual's requirement and the situation.
- One may adopt Theory Z, which suggests that instead of following Theory X or Theory Y, one must assess the situation and act accordingly.
- Herzberg's theory confirms that people value factors like achievement, recognition and challenging work more than things like pay or security.

MOTIVATION: CONTEMPORARY THEORIES

No early theory of motivation could be supported by recent research. This gave birth to various contemporary theories, which are reasonably supported by research findings. Some widely accepted contemporary theories are:

- Clayton Alderfer's Existence, Relatedness & Growth Theory (ERG)
- David McClelland's Three Needs Theory
- Victor Vroom's Expectancy Theory

This does not mean that these contemporary theories are unquestionable or 'perfect' in explaining an individual's motivation. However, these theories explain motivation in the current scenario.

Existence, Relatedness and Growth (ERG) Theory

Clayton Alderfer of Yale University came out with a revised 'need hierarchy'. He propounded three basic groups of core needs, i.e. existence, relatedness and growth, and labelled the theory as ERG theory.

Existence

Physiological and safety needs explained by Maslow are considered here as needs for existence. Every human being has basic material requirements for existence such as, food for hunger, water for thirst, sufficient rest for sleep, house for shelter, clothes for clothing and above all safety, both physical and financial.

Relatedness

Social and ego or esteem needs of Maslow are considered here as relatedness, i.e. the desire to maintain interpersonal relationships by an individual in the society. Every human being wants healthy and meaningful interaction with others.

Growth

According to the ERG theory, every human being has an intrinsic desire for personal development. These include the characteristics which Maslow explained under the categories of esteem and self-actualization.

Conclusion

ERG theory differs from that of Maslow in two aspects. It demonstrates that more than one need may operate at the same time. In addition, it counters Maslow's claim that only when there is a gratification of a lower-level need, the individual starts working towards fulfilling the higher-level need.

According to the ERG theory, an individual can start working on growth needs even though his existence or relatedness needs are unsatisfied. Rather, when an individual fails to fulfil higher-order needs, his desire to work upon a lower-level need increases. Inability to satisfy a need for social interaction, for instance, might increase the desire for earning more money or better working conditions.

> **"A leader is best when people barely know he exists. When his work is done, his aim fulfilled, they will say: We did it ourselves."**
>
> **— Lao-Tzu**

Three Needs Theory

David McClelland proposed the Three Needs Theory (achievement, power and affiliation) for understanding motivation.

Need for Achievement

Human beings have a need to excel, to achieve and to strive in the task on hand. People who have a drive to succeed, according to McClelland, strive for personal achievement rather than the rewards of success. They have an intense desire to do things better or more efficiently than have been done before. These people dislike succeeding by chance. They prefer the challenge that a particular work/job offers and accept responsibility for success or failure. That is the reason they avoid very easy or very difficult tasks. They always set moderately challenging goals with a 50-50 chance of success. They do not get achievement satisfaction if success comes easily. If there is a very high probability of success, it does not challenge their skills.

> **"No motivation or response is animated when the goal is perceived as being virtually or almost impossible."**
>
> **— Unknown**

These people always look for finding solutions to their problems on their own. They expect instant feedback on their performance so that they can come to know whether they are improving or not. They produce better results when given independent charge because they are always interested in how well they do personally rather than influencing others to do well.

Can you identify one of your team members with these characteristics?

Need for Power

Some human beings have the need to exercise power by making others behave in a way that they would like. There is a desire to impact, to influence and to control others. They want to be in charge, and influence others. They prefer to be in situations that are competitive and add to their status. They are more concerned with their own prestige and gaining influence over others rather than with effective performance.

Can you relate this with any of your team members who is actively involved in union activities? His need for power must be very high. He could not satisfy his need in his present role. This must have made him get involved in union activities. What would have happened if you had noticed his need for power and offered him greater responsibilities like addressing his peers during meetings, or doing a special task, such as conducting a market survey or simply a difficult job for which others have reservations?

Need for Affiliation

Human beings desire friendly and close interpersonal relationships. They have a desire to be liked and accepted. They strive for friendship, prefer cooperative situations rather than competitive ones, and desire relationships involving a high degree of mutual understanding.

Recognize your team members who have a high need to achieve and help them set moderately challenging goals. However, if you yourself have a high need to achieve, you may not be able to lead a team successfully.

To be an effective manager you should be high in your need for power, moderate in your need for achievement, and low in your need for affiliation. According to McClelland, "The degree of motivation and efforts rises until the expectancy of success reaches 50 per cent. However, it begins to fall, even though the expectancy of success continues to rise."

Expectancy Theory

According to Victor Vroom, the tendency of a person to act in a certain way depends upon the expectation of the likely outcome that act will generate and on the attractiveness of that outcome to the individual. The Expectancy Theory comprises three variables or relationships.

Attractiveness

It is the importance that the individual places on the expected outcome or reward. The rewards could be some of the unsatisfied needs of the individual.

Performance–Recognition/Reward Linkage

The degree to which an individual believes that performing at a particular level will lead to the attainment of a desired outcome, i.e. expected reward.

Effort–Performance Linkage

It is the individual's perception of the probability that putting a given amount of effort would lead to the expected performance.

An individual before putting an X amount of effort/performance towards the achievement of the organizational goal will consider whether he will be adequately rewarded by the organization to satisfy his individual goals. The perceived outcomes may be positive, such as:

- Pay
- Promotion
- Job security
- Sense of belonging
- Mutual trust
- Fringe benefits
- Opportunity to develop talent or skills
- Congenial relationships

Sometimes the perceived outcomes may be negative, such as:

- Anxiety
- Close supervision
- Threat of dismissal

This may lead to feelings of fatigue, boredom and frustration.

The ultimate motive of every human act is to maximize pleasure and minimize pain.

Conclusion

An essential finding of the Expectancy Theory is that there is no universal principle for explaining everyone's motivations. Therefore, to get the best out of an individual you should understand his goals, the linkage between effort put in by the individual and performance, between performance and rewards, and the importance of the rewards in terms of goal satisfaction.

Make sure that your team members know what is expected out of them and how they will be appraised. It is not enough for you to know that a person wants to satisfy his needs. The individual himself has to perceive high performance as a means to attaining satisfaction and fulfilling needs. Managers often pressurize their subordinates by reminding them of their tasks. However, the result remains abysmal because the individual does not consider the task as important. Therefore, instead of reminding the individual about the task, explain how the task would help him in attaining satisfaction and fulfilling the needs.

The Expectancy Theory explains why in most companies a large segment of the workforce continues to exert minimum effort in carrying out its job responsibilities.

ESSENCE OF MOTIVATIONAL THEORIES

The essence of all the theories is one single fact – what motivates one person does not necessarily motivate another.

No theory is comprehensive enough to explain an individual's motivation. However, the theories help in developing an insight into what motivates or demotivates people. The moment you have this insight you will have at your command the most powerful tool for dealing with human beings.

Before we discuss what motivates people, let us understand what puts them off, in other words demotivates them. This will help us to avoid unknowingly demotivating them.

> **"It doesn't matter how much milk you spill as long as you don't lose the cow."**
>
> **— Harvey Mackay**

POINTS TO REMEMBER

THEORIES OF MOTIVATION

- According to the ERG theory, an individual can start working on growth needs even though his existence or relatedness needs are unsatisfied. Rather, when an individual fails to fulfil his higher-order needs, his desire to work upon a lower-level need increases.
- According to McClelland, to be an effective manager one should be high in need for power, moderate in need for achievement, and low in need for affiliation.
- According to the Three Needs Theory, "The degree of motivation and efforts rises until the expectancy of success reaches 50 per cent. However, it begins to fall, even though the expectancy of success continues to rise."
- According to the Expectancy Theory there is no universal principle for explaining everyone's motivations. To get the best out of an individual one should understand an individual's goals, the linkage between effort put in by the individual and performance, between performance and rewards, and the importance of the rewards in terms of goal satisfaction.
- The essence of all the theories is one single fact – what motivates one person does not necessarily motivate another.

DE
MOTIVATION

How Not to Demotivate

"You can take a horse to the pond, but you cannot make it drink" is an old proverb. A horse can be trained to jump, race, charge into the opposing army, and pull heavy loads. However, the same horse sometimes kicks back, goes in the wrong direction and of course drinks only when it pleases. Therefore, the question why this horse doesn't drink remains pertinent even today. It is true of human beings as well.

Is it a problem or a symptom?

Well, if you lead a horse to the pond and it does not drink, you can be sure that refusing to drink is the symptom, not the problem. The problem could be lack of thirst, stubbornness, fear, or refusing the way you are forcing it to drink.

Similarly, human beings refuse to work or lose interest in performing for various reasons including:

- Lack of interest in the job
- Stubbornness

- Fear of punishment
- Inappropriate rewards
- Conflicting demands or behaviour of the superiors

To find out the reasons that lead to dissatisfaction I asked practising managers from different industries to recall those situations that have dissatisfied them or their team members while performing their day-to-day work. This chapter is a compilation of their responses. I am sure readers will be able to identify and relate with these situations.

Dissatisfying situations act as brakes on human beings and bring them to a standstill. The first time a person encounters such a situation, he may not slow down or stop working. However, the second time, the dissatisfaction gets strengthened and the third time, he stops putting in even his usual efforts. As Herzberg stated, absence of dissatisfaction may not necessarily motivate an individual for producing extraordinary results. Nevertheless, its presence can hold him back or bring him to a complete halt.

A persistent feeling of dissatisfaction gets manifested in the form of demotivation of an individual. It is not necessary that a similar situation will dissatisfy or demotivate an individual. It all depends upon the individual and his response to the situation. However, these situations in isolation or in combination have a potential to precipitate dissatisfaction, concurrently leading to demotivation of an individual.

Therefore, whenever you find a team member refusing to work or comply with your instructions, ponder for a while if he is being subjected to any such situation. The key to get a job done from him will depend upon your ability to remove the brake or obstacle from his path.

"I'm slowly becoming a convert to the principle that you can't motivate people to do things. You can only demotivate them. The primary job of the manager is not to empower but to remove obstacles."

— Scott Adams

DEMOTIVATORS: DUE TO LACK OF PROPER SUPERVISION

We have already discussed that "there are different reasons for different people for the same act". This is because different people have different expectations from their job, seniors or organization. Any mismatch gives rise to conflicting thoughts in their mind. If people are subjected to thoughts that are conflicting with their own opinion, it dissatisfies them. As discussed earlier a persistent feeling of dissatisfaction leads to demotivation.

1. Lack of Direction

According to Victor Vroom's Expectancy Theory, it is the importance of the reward that motivates. If the reward is attractive to the individual, he will certainly put in the best effort. Obviously, he will be interested to know whether the efforts put in are in the right direction. That is the reason people want to know at first what their roles and responsibilities are. Once they start putting their effort, they want to be periodically informed of their progress as to whether they are heading in the right direction or not. On the contrary, if they are not informed about their progress, they will be confused and dissatisfied, and the persistent feeling of dissatisfaction results in demotivation.

Therefore, in order to help your team member derive job satisfaction and remain motivated, it is necessary for you to set the direction for your team members. In other words, you should make sure that at the beginning of a task your team member knows what is expected out of him and how he will be appraised.

Lack of interaction with the 'wise' leads to lack of direction...

2. Lack of Proper Performance Appraisal

Performance appraisal is an important tool for motivating your team members. The objective of performance appraisal is not to criticize the person or to remind him about his duties. According to Victor Vroom's Expectancy Theory, unless the individual himself perceives high performance as a means for attaining satisfaction and fulfilling his needs, he will not put in substantial effort.

If you use performance appraisal as a tool to pressurize people by reminding them of their task, the results may remain abysmal. Therefore, instead of reminding the individual about the actions he should take, explain regularly how these actions would help attain satisfaction and fulfil his needs.

3. Lack of Recognition

According to Herzberg, recognition and reward motivate a person to put in extra effort. Recognition and reward increase the person's self-esteem and create a feeling of accomplishment. However, it is well said that "employees in general remain starved for recognition because their managers are miserly in giving recognition. For want of recognition, productivity of the team members continues to decline and the attrition rate continues to increase."

Reasons for not recognizing people

a. Some managers do not appreciate their subordinates even if they have excelled because they think that the appreciation may make the subordinates high-headed. However, if people do not get recognition when it is due, they get demotivated.
b. Some managers are of the opinion that there is no need to recognize the good efforts of subordinates as they are expected to do good work and are paid for it. They propagate an unsaid philosophy that "until you hear any untoward thing from me, you may take it for granted that you are doing a good job." These managers make a lot of hue and cry on even a small mistake of their team members. Giving negative feedback becomes their habit. Constant negative feedback leads to dissatisfaction and demotivation.

> **"Recognition delayed is recognition denied".**
>
> **— Bhushan**

c. Some managers intentionally deny the recognition to their team members for the simple reason that their managers too denied them the same. However, little do they realize that by denying the recognition to their team members, they themselves are the bigger losers.

d. Some managers consider that offering rewards and recognition is the responsibility of the HR department. They do not spend enough time to observe and measure the efforts of their team members. Most of them do not even know how to recognize an employee. They are afraid of committing a mistake in recognizing the efforts of their people and coming to the notice of their bosses.

It is very easy to "catch somebody doing things wrong". It needs a positive attitude to "catch somebody doing things right".

Recognition and rewards should be used rightly. Many a time managers, to get some extra work from a person, recognize him even if he does not deserve it. This false recognition works the opposite way. Therefore, recognition or a reward should always be appropriate and timely. At the same time, areas where an employee needs to improve should be told to him clearly but separately.

A word of caution:

Never reprimand in public. This affects the individual's self-esteem, whereas recognition should always be made public as it enhances self-esteem.

Another important aspect of recognizing people is that it should match their expectations. Otherwise it may not produce any positive result. Recognizing a person's efforts does not necessarily mean recommending him for promotion. It is observed that most of the times managers encourage a good worker to accept a promotion. It is good; however, if the person instead of considering the promotion as a recognition considers it as a botheration, the very purpose gets defeated. Not every individual looks for promotion; there are a good number of people who want to work for peace of mind rather than career growth. These people may be entrusted some other responsibility rather than being given a promotion. Otherwise, you will "burn the candle at both the ends". On the one hand you will lose a good worker, on the other you may not be able to produce a good manager. Hence, always identify an individual's expectations and show him a clear path for success.

Never offer a reward or recognition to a person which can be perceived as unfair treatment by the other team members; it will be counterproductive.

4. 'Neelkanth' (Lord Shiva)

By nature human beings crave for recognition in the eyes of others. However, quite often managers do it at the cost of their own team members' glory. For any failure they pass on the buck to their subordinates, whereas they try to snatch all the praise for even a small success. We have already discussed that when people are not recognized, they get dissatisfied and in the long run feel demotivated. It is the golden rule of the management: 'Credit is for junior, whereas debit is for the senior.' During '*samudra manthan*' when poison was churned out, it was lord Shiva who kept it in his neck, because of which his neck became blue, and he came to be called 'Neelkanth'. The message to all the practising managers is that you should give credit for a well-accomplished task to your team members, whereas accept any debit in case of their failure. Your team members will not only accept that these results are generated because of the additional efforts put in by you, but also give you credit. You will not only keep your team members motivated, but also command their respect. This feeling will also help you to establish your leadership.

"Respect is the key determinant of high performance leadership. How much people respect you determines how well they perform."

— Brian Tracy

5. Close Supervision

Based on the assumptions of Theory X of Douglas McGregor (i.e. human beings do not like to work and will avoid it whenever possible), some managers have come to believe that "you get only that job done which you inspect." However, the flip side of this statement is also true. Too much inspection only gets the inspected job done but not the expected job from your team member.

> **Too much inspection only gets the inspected job done, but not the expected job from your team member.**

To monitor the efforts of your team members is certainly an important responsibility. However, if you overdo it, you end up doing close supervision. According to Herzberg, close supervision is a hygiene factor and results in dissatisfaction.

a. Close supervision: Reluctance of managers to empower team members

Once again, because of their strong belief in Theory X of Douglas McGregor, some managers rarely share responsibility with their team members or empower them. They never give autonomy (to take his own decisions) to the individual. Ultimately, they end up reminding or questioning every now and then about the completion of the job, which once again amounts to close supervision.

What is worse, managers try to overrule the decisions taken by their subordinates. If a senior manager tries to overrule the decisions taken by the junior manager, it not only demotivates him but also the junior staff. They remain confused as to whose instructions they should follow.

b. Close supervision: Doubt the capabilities/credibility of team members

Both McGregor and Herzberg emphasized that it is the responsibility given to an individual that motivates him. However, in practice it is observed that managers are reluctant to bestow responsibilities to their team members because they do not believe in their capabilities. They always doubt whether their team members are capable of doing what is required of them. This doubt on the capabilities of team members leads to a dilemma, should they offer responsibilities or not. If so, then up to what extent they should do that? Due to this dilemma they neither offer responsibilities nor a sense of accountability to their team members. This lack of responsibility or ambiguous responsibilities demotivates an individual.

Therefore, you must believe in your team members and their capabilities. This requires both intimacy and trust. To develop intimacy you need to get close enough to your team members. A thorough knowledge of their individual nature, likings and preferences will help you to know them well. At the same time this understanding will help you to manage/guide them effectively.

> **"Trust is the emotional glue that binds followers and leaders together."**
>
> **— Unknown**

In order to develop trust you need to be patient. If a team member is not capable at the moment, you must offer time and necessary inputs to assist him. It will be an investment worth millions. You will keep reaping the benefits of it by way of the increased productivity.

A word of caution:

Never substitute your team member. If a team member is not capable of doing a job, instead of substituting him you must help the team member plan the work better, and then based upon the observations made, suggest improvements required for the future task. In teamwork, 1 + 1 should be equal to 11, not just 2. However, when you substitute your team member, the result may be 1 - 1 = 0, and your team member may lose interest in the work itself.

---

c. Close supervision: Doubting the integrity

Sometimes managers doubt the integrity of their team members. This worsens the situation. These managers suspect every move of their team members, and, therefore, follow their activities closely. This once again amounts to close supervision. This does not mean one should ignore the actions of an individual whose integrity is doubtful. If you doubt, investigate thoroughly and if the person is found guilty, take appropriate action immediately. Be subtle in the investigation. Take prompt action to avoid carrying on the suspicion to other team members leading to the dissatisfaction and demotivation of the whole team.

> **"Integrity is like virginity, once lost, lost forever."**
>
> **— Dr. Kurien**

d. Close supervision: Freedom to perform

Another reason for close supervision is the mindset of managers towards people. They expect the people to be always correct and make no mistakes. They scold their subordinates for even small mistakes. The subordinates become apprehensive and lose the spirit of experimenting. They become inhibited, gradually lose interest in the job, and ultimately get demotivated.

'Freedom to perform' may pose a lot more problems than you know. However, managing those problems or problematic team members is not as difficult as dealing with the problem of getting the demotivated subordinate to perform.

Whatever the reason, close supervision leads to dissatisfaction among team members that eventually leads to demotivation.

> **"If you bake bread with indifference, you bake bitter bread that feeds but half man's hunger".**
>
> **— Kahlil Gibran**

e. Close supervision: Forcing people to work in their (manager's) way

Lack of freedom to perform has another implication. Some managers are not only reluctant to offer freedom to perform, but also force their team members to work according to their method. Most of the time people do not resist the work they are assigned but resist working the way they are forced to work. You will find the story given below not only interesting but also absolutely apt for human beings.

There was a couple who did not have children. Hence, they bought a pet, a puppy dog. Since they had no child, they were very attached to the puppy. They wanted him to be healthy, and therefore used to take care of him and provide good food. Someone suggested to them that if they gave cod-liver oil to the puppy, it would become robust. They bought the oil and started giving it daily. It was very difficult for them to make the puppy drink the ▶

oil, as it used to jump and run around. Therefore,the husband used to catch the puppy between his legs and the wife used to pour the oil in its mouth with the help of a big funnel.

One day while making the puppy drink, some oil got spilled on the ground. While the wife went to bring something to clean the ground, to their surprise they found the puppy licking the oil from the ground. That day they realized the fact that the dog never disliked drinking the oil but was resisting the way they were making him drink the oil.

6. Company's Policies

According to Herzberg, company policies are one of the common causes of employee demotivation. Company policies are prepared for employees in general. They cannot, therefore, satisfy everybody or may not be applicable in all situations. If a particular policy creates dissatisfaction, managers find themselves helpless. Sometimes neither the dissatisfied person nor the manager has understood a policy correctly. Therefore, there is a need to understand and interpret company policies correctly in the context of the existing situation to the person concerned.

Raghav and Sunit were both working in a large pharmaceutical company. Their headquarters was in Kanpur, a pool territory of three representatives. Every promotional cycle of three months (90 days), the company used to have an incentive plan. Even though they had a vacancy for one representative at Kanpur, they used to earn a lot of incentives. Just before the beginning of new financial year Raghav got promoted as Frontline Manager based at Kanpur HQ.

Immediately after his promotion he selected Sanjay as his replacement. Within a short time he filled in the vacancy of another MR at Kanpur. By the time the new representative Rajeev joined territory, the promotional cycle already had started. According to the company rule, in order to be eligible for incentive one must have worked for a minimum of 75 days during a particular cycle. In case a person joins in between a cycle, he will get 40 per cent of the incentive amount, whereas the one who is working before the cycle started will be eligible for 60 per cent of incentive amount.

Kanpur pool once again qualified for an incentive amount of Rs. 15,000/person. By virtue of working for more than 75 days both Sanjay and Rajeev qualified for the incentive. However, according to the company's policy, Sunit and Sanjay were disbursed Rs. 22,000/ whereas Rajeev got only Rs. 8,000/. The moment Raghav received the incentive circular he could foresee the anomaly. He realized that even after receiving Rs. 22,000/- Sanjay might not necessarily be as motivated as Rajeev will be demotivated. He for sure knew that the efforts put in by both were almost equal.

Hence, he suggested that the company distribute the amount equally between both of them. The company did listen to his suggestion and deducted Rs. 7,000/ from Sanjay and paid it to Rajeev. This saved Rajeev from getting demotivated by wrong interpretation of the company policy.

7. Conflicting Expectations of Superiors

According to a law of physics, whenever two forces are applied on a single object, it is the direction and the strength of individual forces that decide the resultant force applicable on the object (direction and strength of the resultant force). For example, force A has an intrinsic strength of say 2 units, whereas force B has the strength of 3 units. Both the forces are working upon object O from two different directions as shown in the figure. Ultimately the effect of force on the object O, i.e. the resultant force, will be diagonal to the direction of forces A and B. Moreover, the strength of this resultant force will be less than the sum of their individual strengths. In this case, it will be less than 5.

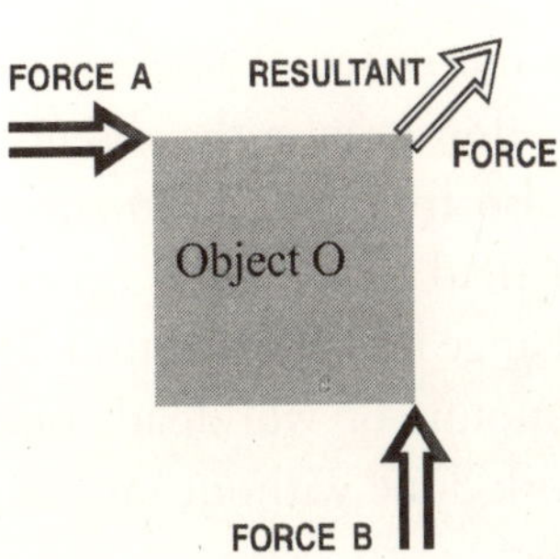

On the contrary, if both the forces act upon the object in the same direction, the resultant force will be in the same direction and the strength of the resultant force will be the sum total of their individual strengths, i.e. 5.

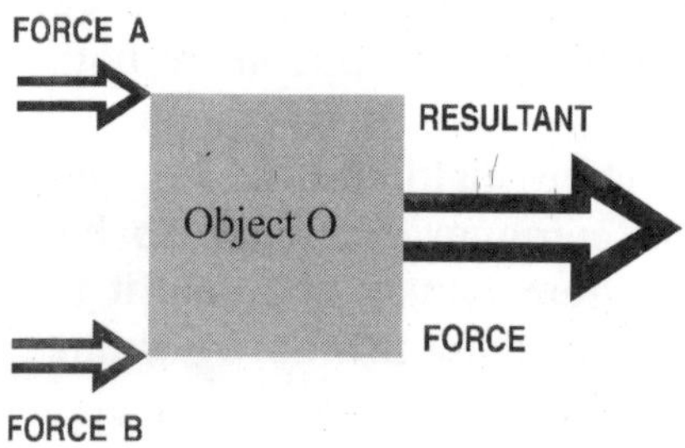

Most of the time, managers have conflicting expectations from the same person. They not only give different instructions for implementing the company's strategy (sometimes contradictory to each other or their own instructions given earlier), but also compel the subordinate to work according to their instructions only. Conflicting instructions of superiors confuse the person about which instruction he should follow. Ultimately he resorts to an entirely different action, which does not conform to any of the instructions given. Therefore, while giving an instruction to a person, keep in mind that the instruction does not contradict the instructions of your senior, company or that given by you earlier.

8. Monotony of Work

According to Herzberg, work itself is the biggest motivator. If one enjoys his work he never gets tired. Rather, he puts extra effort even in the absence of motivators. However, the flip side of this is also true. The moment a person loses interest in his job he starts feeling tired or becomes upset. Even the presence of other motivators may not change his state of mind. It is true that a person is not tired due to the amount of workload, but because of the lack of interest in the job. Any work done without interest never produces expected results.

> **"If you grudge the crushing of the grapes, your grudge distils a poison in the wine".**
>
> **— Kahlil Gibran**

Monotony of work can lead to boredom. Doing the same job for days, weeks, and months and years, people develop an aversion to work. This is natural and might be true for you as well. Here comes the role of empathy. If monotony is leading to lack of interest in the work, you must try to break it. It might be through requesting the HR department for job rotation or realigning the job responsibilities of your team members within your group. Another way to break monotony is to take your team members with their families on weekends or holidays. This will serve a dual purpose; it will break the monotony, and at the same time it will bring you all closer to one another.

9. Working Conditions

Herzberg labelled working conditions as hygiene factors. 'Working condition' is an umbrella term. Apart from the hygiene factors discussed earlier, the physical set-up for working, i.e. from the place to sit, airconditioning, equipments such as computer, printer, xerox machine and fax, adds to the working conditions. Inappropriate or a faulty set-up leads to dissatisfaction.

Similarly, for people working alone, living away from their family, working without a counsellor itself is a dissatisfying experience. On top of it, facing reluctance, insincerity, rude behaviour, tight schedules or odd hours of working or getting calls from customers, coupled with atmospheric conditions, poor mode of transportation or communication, etc. make him dissatisfied.

In addition, if a person misses a promotion or an incentive, he feels further dissatisfied. Persistent dissatisfaction coupled with some of the above-mentioned circumstances can certainly lead to demotivation and low performance.

10. Lack of Communication

Quite often managers assume that people would come to know on their own about the developments/changes that have been brought into practice.

They don't realize the fact that if important information/development is not shared at the proper time, it will lead to frustration among the team members. On the contrary, if the information about the changes is communicated in time, people can plan their activities and work better. Their approach will be more objective and focused and will certainly yield higher results.

One fine morning while entering into the office, Rajiv did not find the same level of enthusiasm in the morning greeting of Lokesh. This despite the fact that Lokesh had bagged an order worth Rs. 5 lakhs from one of the most prestigious customers in the city a day before. During the next few hours of the day, Lokesh's behaviour was erratic and Rajiv could sense something unusual. Rajiv called Lokesh for an informal meeting to enquire what had gone wrong....

While discussing, Lokesh informed Rajiv that the product for which Lokesh had struck the deal the previous day, had been discontinued by the head office product team about a week back. However, there was no communication sent by the product team either to the field personnels or to the regional managers. As a result all the hard work that Lokesh carried out during the last two weeks chasing this customer had gone down the drain. Moreover, nobody in the company had the courage to face the customer or to return the cheque of Rs. 50,000/ which Lokesh had collected as a confirmation of the order.

11. Lack of Empathy

Remember people act and react on what they believe is good and is in their self-interest. Often people get so involved with themselves or their ideas that they are unwilling to view the idea or situation from the other person's point of view. Empathy means wearing the shoes of the other person, in other words, seeing from the other person's point of view. Empathy does not mean that you have to always agree with the other's point of view. It is to understand why the other person behaved so. Once you start empathizing with others you realize that often the cause of the dispute is lack of understanding between you and the other person. Remember, lack of empathy leads to misunderstanding between you and your team members that eventually leads to demotivation.

Take the example mentioned earlier in this chapter, of a person subjected to poor physical or psychological working conditions. He is bound to get dissatisfied. It is observed that most of the practising managers remain insensitive to these issues. They know that the working conditions cannot be improved, as they are beyond their control. Some of them even want their subordinates to accept these conditions as normal since, they themselves consider it normal. However, it does not happen that way. People may not verbalize their resentment, yet they will not feel comfortable working under those conditions. Similarly, when people face one or other psychological conditions mentioned earlier while working, they feel dissatisfied. Here comes the role of empathy. Once you put yourself in your team member's shoes, you start appreciating the hardships they face and will be in a position to provide them with the appropriate solution. Many a time you may not be in a position to change the conditions or do something for their problems, yet if you can just listen to their problems, it will reduce their level of dissatisfaction.

POINTS TO REMEMBER

DEMOTIVATORS: DUE TO LACK OF SUPERVISION

- In order to help team members derive job satisfaction and remain motivated, it is necessary to set the direction for team members.
- The objective of performance appraisal is not to criticize the person or to remind him about duties. It is an important tool for motivating an individual.
- Recognition and reward motivates a person to put in extra efforts.
- Recognition and reward increases the person's self-esteem and creates a feeling of accomplishment.
- One should give credit for a well-accomplished task to the team members, whereas accept any debit in case of their failure.
- To monitor the efforts of team members is certainly an important responsibility. However, if it is overdone, it may amount to close supervision.
- People do not resist the work they are assigned but refuse to work in the way they are forced to work.
- There is a need to understand and interpret company policies in the context of the existing situation correctly to the person concerned.
- While giving instruction to a person, keep in mind that the instruction should not contradict the instructions of a senior, company or that given by oneself earlier.
- Monotony of work may lead to the lack of interest in the work, which leads to individual's demotivation.
- Inappropriate physical set-up for working, i.e. the place to sit, air-conditioning, equipments such as computer, printer, xerox machine, fax, leads to dissatisfaction. That consequently leads to demotivation.
- Lack of empathy leads to misunderstanding between the manager and the team members, which eventually leads to demotivation.

DEMOTIVATORS: DUE TO POOR 'ON-THE-JOB PERFORMANCE'

Values influence an individual's attitude. The attitude towards the job decides the level of performance as well as satisfaction. If an individual's values conflict with those of his organization, he may be a misfit in the organization. He will put in effort but that effort may not yield the results expected of him. This persistent feeling of misfit over a period demotivates the person. Let's see how poor performance may lead to the demotivation.

1. Poor Performance

According to Herzberg, sense of achievement itself motivates a person. The opposite is also true. As long as your team members are achieving their goals, they will be motivated to plan for the next higher goal. However, the day they fail, they will feel dissatisfied and demotivated. If the performance of a team member continues to be low month after month, he will certainly get demotivated. Often managers start neglecting these people, further complicating the situation and leading to their lack of confidence.

Sometimes managers start planning to remove such demotivated employees from the company. Instead of finding out the reason for low performance, managers want the person to be removed. What is the guarantee that the replacement will produce better results? Hence, instead of removing, facilitate the subordinate's job so that he achieves success and remains motivated.

> **"Striving for excellence motivates; striving for perfection is demoralizing."**
>
> **— Harriet Brailker**

2. Sales Territory

Every sales territory has its peculiarities. Some territories have more potential than others. Some are easy to cover due to the geographic spread. Some territories, because of their location, have inherent distribution problems like goods not reaching in time, or some of the markets being covered by the wholesalers of nearby territories or infiltration of goods from the adjacent territories. Similarly, if the territory has been covered well in the past, the new salesperson gets positive reception from the customer. On the contrary, if the territory has not been covered well, the new salesperson gets a negative reception. These problems of territory amount to working conditions. As discussed earlier, inappropriate working conditions lead to dissatisfaction.

Hence, your endeavour should be to help your team member find out a solution to these problems. Alternatively, if either of you is unable to find a solution or you know that there can be no solution to a particular problem, you need to counsel your team member. Lack of proper counselling may further aggravate the situation, which may result in demotivation.

> **"Sales is a person-to-person business. You cannot send the sales manual out to make the sale. Sales manuals have no legs and no voice."**
>
> **— Jim Rohn**

3. Target

Budgeting for the year is much more than merely calculating growth given by the company and distributing according to the territory's contribution. While allocating targets to individual territories, often managers ignore factors that have a direct bearing on the performance of a territory. If the targets are set without understanding the ground realities, wrong targeting and lopsided performance of territories takes place. Naturally, the person who faces the brunt of the attack gets demotivated.

4. Low Expectations

Your team members' performance to a great extent depends upon what you expect from them and how you treat them. Therefore, your success is directly proportionate to your ability to create high performance expectations from your team members. On the contrary, if your expectation falls short of that of your team members, it demotivates them. Consequently, their productivity starts declining.

One of the reasons for low expectation is the manager's fear of failure. However, just because you do not want your team member to fail, aiming low is not the answer. Even if one achieves this goal, it is a failure. U.N. Mehta, the founder chairman, Torrent Group, rightly said, "It is pardonable to aim high and miss, however, aiming low is absolutely unpardonable."

Managers who have faith in their team and in its capabilities always have high expectations. While selecting, training and motivating team members, they always keep high expectations, and their expectation always yields higher returns.

> **"It is pardonable to aim high and miss, however, aiming low is absolutely unpardonable."**
>
> **— U.N. Mehta**

Power of expectation

It is almost impossible for you to mask your expectation. The irony is that directly or indirectly, negative or low expectations are communicated much faster than positive or high expectations. However, the most dangerous is the silent treatment knowingly or unknowingly given by most of the managers. If you fail to openly communicate your expectations to your team members, you still communicate negative feelings or low expectations.

Nevertheless, expectations should not be unrealistically high. Failure of subordinates to meet the unrealistically high expectations not only demotivates them but also prevents them from accepting future challenges.

5. Fear of Failure

Human nature does not accept rejection or failure. Even the thought of encountering rejection or failure creates fear in the human mind and inhibits people from taking action. The feeling of rejection originates from the word NO. This NO may be just a negation of the point or the proposal and not of the person. However, people take it that it is not their proposal but they themselves have been rejected. This feeling of rejection leads to demotivation. Hence, instead of shouting, you need to counsel your team member and encourage him to find out the reasons for the failure. Once the person realizes that it is his mistake that is responsible for his failure, he will take corrective action on his own.

> **"To handle yourself, use your head; to handle others, use your heart."**
>
> **— Donald Laird**

☑ POINTS TO REMEMBER

DEMOTIVATORS: DUE TO POOR ON-THE-JOB PERFORMANCE

- If people achieve their goals, they feel motivated to plan for the next higher goal.
- If the targets are set without understanding the ground realities, wrong targeting and lopsided performance of territories takes place. The person who faces the brunt of the attack gets demotivated.
- People's performance to a great extent depends upon what is expected from them and how one treats them.
- A manager's success is directly proportionate to the ability to create high performance expectations from the team members.
- Instead of shouting, one needs to counsel team members and encourage them to find out the reasons for their failure. Once the person realizes it is his own mistake that is responsible for his failure, he will take corrective action on his own.

DEMOTIVATORS: DUE TO INAPPROPRIATE LEADERSHIP STYLE

1. Unfulfilled Promises

According to Victor Vroom's Expectancy Theory, people act in a certain way depending upon the expectation of the likely outcome that act will generate and on the attractiveness of that outcome to the individual. An individual, before putting a particular amount of effort towards the achievement of the organizational goal, always considers whether he will be adequately rewarded by the organization by way of increase in salary or a promotion.

Many a time it is observed that managers take undue advantage of this by making false promises. They feel by doing so they will be motivating an individual for better performance. Nevertheless, it works as 'showing a carrot to a donkey'. What they don't realize is that even a donkey doesn't run after the carrot if it doesn't get one to eat. Similarly, a false promise may motivate a person momentarily. The moment he realizes that he is being cheated, his enthusiasm suddenly evaporates and brings him to a standstill. Just like an engine, if a human being comes to a standstill, it is very difficult to restart him. Another drawback of a false promise is that it may make a person complacent.

I know an excellent sales representative who started performing right from the first month of his joining the company. Within the first year he had been rated as one of the top performers of his region. His superior, in order to ("so called") motivate him, gave him the assurance that he will be the next person to be promoted from his team. He even started sending him circulars meant for managers.

On another occasion, when the company was finding it difficult to handle certain IR issues, he used that sales representative for counselling his colleagues in other territories. This undue recognition at the early stage of his career gave him a sense of euphoria. The importance and the recognition, which was given to him to motivate him further, ultimately spoiled him.

By the time he had completed two years in the company, he started visualizing himself as a manager and became complacent. Subsequently when he was not offered the promotion as he was lacking other qualities required for being an effective manager, he got frustrated. In the bargain, the company lost both a good representative and a future manager.

2. Denying a Promotion or Transfer Because the Person is Producing Extraordinary Results

Every manager wants to have a team of people who are good, hard-working, sincere and productive. However, when they have such a team member, they become selfish. They don't want that member to leave them. It may be due to a transfer to some other place/department or a promotion. They carry a fear that if this person leaves them, the new incumbent may not produce as good results as the earlier person was producing. In order to retain this person they try to manipulate the information and, convey wrong feedback to seniors. What they forget is that they can retain a person physically not mentally. The day the person comes to know that he is being retained just because he is producing good results, his enthusiasm decreases. A feeling of being cheated develops, which stops him from making efforts that were producing extraordinary results. Ultimately, when he does not get transferred to the place of his choice or does not get promoted, demotivation sets in.

"It is easy to fool yourself. It is more difficult to fool the people you work for. It is still more difficult to fool the people you work with. And it is impossible to fool the people who work under your direction."

— Unknown

3. Lack of Interpersonal Relationship

According to McClelland, human beings desire friendly and close interpersonal relationships. They have a desire to be liked and accepted. They strive for friendship, prefer cooperative situations rather than competitive ones, and desire relationships involving a high degree of mutual understanding. A leader who fails to provide such an environment to his team members certainly disappoints them. A persistent feeling of disappointment leads to demotivation.

Therefore, in order to save your team members from getting disappointed or demotivated you must develop an emotional bond among your team members. To be a part of a team is like being a part of a family, where every team member respects and values the opinions of other members. There is mutual trust among the team members. People value the individual's suggestions, communicate openly, manage differences, share successes and welcome ideas even from a new member.

TIPS FOR DEVELOPING STRONG INTERPERSONAL RELATIONSHIPS

- You must find time and invite your team members for a social gathering every now and then.
- During these gatherings you should avoid any shop talk.
- You should also forget for a while that you are their boss. You must act like one of them.
- During other occasions when they want to discuss their personal matters, you must take genuine interest in their problem. What is more important is to give them a patient hearing rather than a desired solution.

We will discuss at length the tips for developing strong interpersonal relationships under the topic Team Building.

4. Conflicting Behaviours of Superiors

Sometimes managers tell their team members to do a task. Then they lay down policies, procedures, and rules that prevent the person from carrying out the task or delay the performance. For example, they ask people to be innovative. However, when their team member turns up with an idea that seems to be radical, they don't allow any deviation from the listed norms. Little do they realize, that without any deviation from the norms, how one can invent a new method for doing the same job. Every time, if people encounter such a situation, they get dejected and ultimately stop trying.

Sometimes managers tell their team members that they want cooperation from each one of them. Subsequently, they reward the selfish behaviour of an individual. Such actions demotivate other team members.

Often, managers propagate an idea as it is the fairest of all, however when they reward their favourites, they create dissatisfaction among the other team members. In the end the team members lose faith in the system and the superiors.

5. Feeling of Favouritism

According to Herzberg, timely and appropriate recognition is a powerful motivator. However, often people are promoted depending on who they are rather than what they have done. This form of favouritism demotivates the other team members. This feeling of favouritism applies not only to promotions but also to small rewards or recognitions.

Sometimes when a senior manager changes company, he takes along the whole team. Both companies do not necessarily gain out of it. One company loses good people. The second company gets people whose loyalty is to the manager, not to the organization. The team may repeat its act with the new organization as well. Moreover, a feeling of favouritism sets in the organization/team and makes other members frustrated and demotivated.

6. Comparing Two Individuals

Comparing two individuals always leads to a distaste in one who is not found up to the mark or as good as his counterpart. When you compare two individuals, the self-esteem of the one found inferior is affected. He not only loses his position in the eyes of others, but his own self-respect diminishes. He develops sour feelings for both you and his counterpart. If he is subjected to similar sour feelings quite often, it will make him dissatisfied and may become a cause for his demotivation. Therefore, as far as possible you should avoid comparison of two individuals. You may give examples of another person but in such a way that it does not amount to direct comparison.

7. Denying Leave

It is a very touchy subject. As a senior you have the authority to grant or say 'no' to your team member's request for leave. There is no hard and fast rule for accepting or refusing leaves. However, one thing is certain; the moment a person applies for leave he starts preparing mentally for utilizing his leave. It might be a just one day's casual leave or 15 days privilege leave. A negation to his request comes as a sudden block to his pleasant thoughts, which is very difficult for him to accept. In most cases it leads to a distaste between both of you. Once you refuse the leave, you may find him physically present but mentally absent. Needless to mention, mere physical presence does not get work done. The very purpose of refusing leave – that he will work productively – gets defeated. Work exigencies may sometimes warrant the presence of a person on the day he has asked for leave. In such situations you need to counsel and explain why you need him at work on that day.

On certain occasions it might so happen that one of your team members asks for leave in advance. However, his presence is a must for the completion of a particular task. You have two options, one to refuse and another to accept. In both the cases work will suffer. If you accept his request, he will not be there to perform. Alternatively, if you refuse, he may not put in his best, as he would be upset. In such situations you must take advantage of the individual's motivation. You may ask him to complete the task on or before the date he is scheduled to leave. In most cases it will so happen that he delivers much more than what you expected; that too much before the scheduled time for the completion of task. This is the power of motivation.

8. Being a Workaholic

It is observed that some over-enthusiastic managers become workaholics. They not only enjoy working long hours, but also want their team members to work extra hours. There is no harm in asking people to put in extra hours if there is a need. However, it is observed that some managers enjoy sitting late in office. They spend their day attending to trivial issues or jobs, and remember the important tasks only towards the end of the day. A subordinate may do extra hours of work if the work is important enough. Nevertheless, if it is a routine, it frustrates people.

Jaya, a smart girl, was jubilant about joining a five-star hotel as receptionist. Her dream of meeting celebrities, people of repute and from the high end of the society came true. She was highly enthusiastic about her job and within no time she was considered as one of the best receptionists of the hotel. However, her decision to quit the job came as a shock to everyone.

The reason for her extreme step was the one mentioned above. Her boss, the Front Office Supervisor, was very happy as she used to manage all the problems/situations herself. Nevertheless, this became a problem for her as almost everyday he started expecting her to be on the job even after the scheduled duty time. On one or the other pretext he used to keep her working late. A day came when she gave up and resigned.

Similarly, asking people to work on Sundays or holidays also leads to dissatisfaction. Once in a while you may ask people to come on holidays for work. However, if you do it often, it leads to dissatisfaction. From the moment you call them they get disturbed and keep thinking only negative about you and the work. Their resentment is reflected in their job as well. Therefore, as far as possible, avoid asking people to work extra hours or on Sundays or holidays. Rather, you should work upon improving your time management.

9. Being Partial

Remember, your success depends upon the performance of all your team members and not of only a few extraordinary members. However, it is observed that most managers develop some affection for some team members. No doubt, these members are good as far as their competence or skills are concerned. Nevertheless, they alone cannot help you succeed in your objective unless the rest of the team produces what is expected out of them. Hence, giving undue acknowledgement or appreciation to any one's contribution may not necessarily produce desired results because it may cause dissatisfaction among others. A persistent feeling of dissatisfaction will demotivate other team members, which will nullify the results produced by those select few. Therefore, be impartial with your team members.

> **"If an employee gets a raise when he did nothing to deserve it, you will probably have ten disgruntled employees".**
>
> **— Unknown**

Similarly, while giving feedback to the higher management you should be impartial. You must give the factual and correct feedback. Managers often twist facts or findings in favour of their favourites. Once again, by doing so in the long run you create problems for yourself. Those members, whose feedback is not positive, will face the brunt of higher management's displeasure. This will make them unhappy. What is worse, many a time directly or indirectly juniors come to know about the feedback given by you. If this happens, you not only demotivate them, but also lose respect in their eyes. This will be a disaster. It will be difficult for you to salvage your lost respect or leadership.

10. Asking People to Do What You Wouldn't Like to Do Yourself

Often it is observed that managers ask their team members to do something that they themselves wouldn't like to do. For example, working till late hours, asking people to work on holidays, taking work home and so on. Similarly, they object to the juniors doing things which they themselves often do. For example, wearing a particular dress during duty hours or not wearing a necktie or coming late to office, while they themselves are often late. Juniors may not react or do anything against such seniors; however, seniors lose an opportunity to command respect from them. It also demotivates them.

One day a lady took her son to a saint and asked him, "Guruji, my son eats a lot of sweets. Please tell him not to do so." Guruji after listening to her asked her to come after 15 days. After 15 days the lady once again came with a lot of hope to guruji's hut. Guruji once again asked her to come after 15 days. She went back. After one month she came again to guruji's hut. The saint called his son and asked him to sit close to him. Then he told him the various disadvantages of taking sweets in high quantities.

To the lady's surprise from that day onward the boy stopped consuming sweets at all. The lady was extremely happy and went back to the same saint to thank him. She said, "Guruji, thank you very much. Your few sentences have done a miracle, my son has stopped eating sweets. But I have a question. When you were to say only a few sentences, then why did you take one month to say that?" "Because I myself used to eat a lot of sweets," the Guruji replied.

11. Lack of Support

Human beings want a predictable, orderly world with an uninterrupted routine or rhythm. Any confrontation, injustice, unfairness or inconsistency makes them feel endangered. In today's fast pace of life most people feel lonely. They don't have a friend with whom they can share their successes and failures. However, when they are stuck on a personal or professional issue, they look to their seniors for support.

In such a case, what is important is your willingness to help your team members and not necessarily the desired help. Your team members are aware of your limitations and expect you to at least try to help. Lack of support certainly demotivates a person, whereas timely support reinforces the sense of belonging.

Sanjay was transferred to a new area as Frontline Manager. Most of his representatives were highly involved in union activities. One of his team members, Ramesh, who was previously his classmate, was a hard-working and sincere representative. While analysing his territory sales, Sanjay realized that his performance had declined in the recent past. During a visit to Ramesh's

territory, Sanjay made it a point to discuss the reason for the drop in performance. Since, he knew him well, he was anticipating a warm welcome during his first visit to the territory. On the contrary, it came to him as a surprise when he saw Ramesh coming without a bike for joint fieldwork. He presumed that it might be under repair. They worked the whole day in the field; during work Sanjay noticed Ramesh's indifferent attitude.

During his second visit to the territory, Sanjay once again found Ramesh coming without his bike. On being asked, Ramesh gave a strange reason. He said, "These days petrol is very costly." Sanjay again found his attitude indifferent. Sanjay could make out that there was something wrong. He called Ramesh for dinner the same night to find out the reason. However, Ramesh did not give any reason. While having dinner Sanjay casually remarked, "You do not put your heart into work, otherwise you can do miracles". This worked as a trigger. Ramesh just burst out, "How do you expect me to put my heart into work when there is nobody in the company to look after me?" Then Ramesh told him his story.

Ramesh was posted in a town other than his hometown. Once he had some arguments with his landlord, who was a very influential person of that town. The landlord asked him to vacate the house immediately, failing which he would have to face untoward consequences. He gave a frantic call to his then Frontline Manager, Sanjay's predecessor, for help. The Frontline Manager, instead of counselling him, did not even bother to call him back or visit his territory. Of course, with the intervention of a few leading persons of the town, the matter got settled, however it left a scar on Ramesh's heart. This was one of the reasons Ramesh joined the union later on.

This is an apt example of how lack of support can lead to demotivation.

12. Ridiculing Ideas

Don't ridicule the ideas of your team members however silly they may be. Ridiculing not only demotivates a person in carrying out his present job, but also affects his future endeavours. Remember, all the great researchers, when they first announced their discoveries and inventions, were ridiculed. Thank heavens, the scientists did not stop their research. However, your team members may not be as motivated as those scientists were.

13. Public Reprimand

Reprimanding in front of others often leads to demotivation, losing self-respect, and respect in the eyes of others. Often senior managers criticize or reprimand junior managers in front of their team members. Such a behaviour, in the long run, demotivates the junior managers and creates problems for the senior managers as well. Junior managers not only lose self-respect, but also respect of their team members. Even routine matters are directly referred to senior managers. This not only increases the workload of senior managers but further demotivates the junior managers.

> **"When an employee gets a dressing down for something he didn't do, the morale of the entire group is affected."**
>
> **— Unknown**

Often this is one of the reasons why good workers leave the company. The first time, the person may not leave, but a thought gets planted. The second time, the thought gets strengthened, and the third time, he starts looking for another job. Imagine the loss your company has to suffer when such people take away with them the wealth of knowledge, experience and contacts with the customers, often, straight to the competition. Therefore, you must avoid any such situation that may lead you towards reprimanding a person in public.

> **"When an employee makes a mistake, it should be brought to his attention, acknowledged by him, and then put aside. Mistakes are opportunities to learn and not to beat the pride or self-respect out of people".**
>
> **— Unknown**

14. Motivation or Manipulation

Motivation means getting somebody to do something because he wanted to do it and not because you wanted him to do it. The latter is known as manipulation and not motivation. When people get to know that their abilities are not being utilized properly, they develop a negative feeling about their job, seniors or even career. Similarly, when they find their seniors, instead of trying to develop their capabilities, are forcing them to continue doing mundane jobs, they lose interest. A persistent negative feeling about the job or career leads to demotivation.

> **"Leadership is the art of getting someone else to do something you want done because he wants to do it."**
>
> **— General Dwight David Eisenhower**

15. No Future Prospects in the Organization

Most companies have a system of internal promotions. Yet people are inducted from outside the organization at higher positions. The top management's reason for inducting from outside is that the company does not have the required job knowledge/skill/maturity among its people. The question arises as to whose responsibility it is to develop people's job knowledge/skill/maturity. What have the managers and the management done to train their own people?

The individual who wants to make a career in the organization loses hope of being rewarded. He gets demotivated and leaves the organization.

16. Feeling of Insignificance

Teams always consist of a few extraordinary performers, whom we call achievers, a few mediocre ones, and a few laggards. Success of the team depends not only upon the results of the achievers but also on those of the mediocres and laggards. Achievers always excel because of their internal motivation. They do not wait for somebody to tell or remind them. However, the same is not true of the mediocres and laggards; they not only require to be reminded, but also pushed.

Often the mediocre and laggards are neglected because of the manager's reluctance to put in efforts to develop them. This feeling of neglect leads not only to their dissatisfaction, but also demotivates them further. If nurtured properly, these people not only repay your investment by producing better results, but also stick with the company for long.

> **"Respect a man, he will do more."**
> **— James Howell**

17. Lack of Confidence

The genesis of lack of confidence lies in early childhood conditioning. In early childhood, when the child is unable to walk, everybody encourages the child to walk or at least stand. Everybody is positive, "Yes, you can do this." The child is rewarded with positive reinforcement in the form of hugging and kissing. However, when the child starts walking, the suggestions become negative, such as, be careful, do not do this, or do not touch it. Of course, this reflects the caring attitude of parents, but these statements of caution condition the raw mind of a child with negative impressions. These negative impressions finally lead to lack of confidence.

Similarly, if you also give negative suggestions or instructions to your team members, you will make them inhibited and over a period of time make them lose their confidence. Lack of confidence can also be due to the negative experience of past. People who failed in a particular act are always reminded of the negative result at the time of future attempts. Lack of confidence also comes from lack of knowledge of the work or what is expected out of them. Whatever the reason, persistent lack of confidence leads to demotivation. Therefore, instead of giving negative suggestions, you must try to help your team members to improve their competencies. This will help them boost their confidence.

18. Negative Opinions

Negative opinion of others contributes to a negative self-image and leads to loss of confidence and morale, ultimately leading to demotivation. Once you develop a negative opinion about a person you always find fault with him. It is like viewing through coloured glasses when every object looks coloured. Therefore, even though the individual may not be guilty, you will always blame him. Your negative opinion may compel your team member to think negative. Over a time he may develop a feeling that he is not wanted in the organization. Needless to mention, this feeling will lead to further negative thoughts about you and the organization, which will be counterproductive. What is more harmful is that the victim not only becomes negative, but also spreads negative feelings among other team members.

19. Frequent Changes in Standard Operating Procedures

Standard Operating Procedures are the procedures that need to be implemented during a full year, or in some cases forever, that too without any change. However, it is observed that senior managers incorporate new procedures every now and then. Any change in the working routine upsets a person. It is observed that when a senior manager joins a new organization, he expects people to immediately start implementing what was being done in his earlier organization, without realizing that this is a different environment; not only the people, but also their working style and thought processes are different. Till the time they accept him, it will be very difficult for them to accept his ideas. However, his insistence leads to their half-hearted implementation, which never produces the expected results. Hence, it is suggested that instead of adding new procedures one should try to find out the merits of the old ones. Instead of changing a procedure completely it is better to bring modifications in the existing procedures that may deliver better results.

20. Lack of Delegation

Delegation is handing over the task to your team members and then helping them to match or exceed your standards. Delegation helps your team members develop their skills and gain experience. At the same time it helps to create time for you to concentrate on important long-term matters such as strategic planning and training. However, it is observed that managers do delegate the job to their subordinates, but every now and then they keep asking about the implementation or the outcome. This defeats the very purpose of delegation.

No doubt, control is an integral part of delegation. However, questioning every now and then not only irritates your team members, but also gives them an impression that you do not have confidence in them. In the long run it leaves them with a feeling of dissatisfaction. Instead, it is better to determine the methodology for monitoring the progress. The same should be informed to your team members well in advance. You can monitor the progress with a well-defined report, periodical face-to-face meetings, and by observing their performance. This will not only save your team members from getting dissatisfied, but also help them to derive a sense of accomplishment periodically.

One more point, which you must keep in your mind while delegating is the task maturity of your team members. Accordingly, you should decide the extent to which you can delegate tasks to a particular team member and the type of controls you need to monitor the progress. Many a time, it is observed that managers treat all their team members alike. This frustrates a particular team member whose task maturity is high. He considers it a lack of faith in his capabilities, which demotivates him further. Needless to mention, displaying favouritism while delegating dissatisfies or frustrates people.

TIPS FOR DELEGATING WITHOUT FRUSTRATING YOUR TEAM MEMBERS

- You must be clear about your team members' roles.
- You must set challenging tasks and amibitious goals for each of your team members.
- You must assign jobs based on the task maturity of your team members.
- You must assign only those jobs to your team members which you yourself would like to do.
- You must consider your team members competent workers.
- You must create a positive work environment that is flexible.
- You must offer your team members all the necessary support.
- You must use all channels to communicate with your team members.
- You must encourage your team members to speak out what they deem correct.
- You must remember that trust is a two-way process; it takes time and effort to get established.
- You must avoid any such act that can display favouritism.

> **"Never keep work simply because you do it better. Leadership involves handing over the task to others, and then helping them to match or exceed your standards."**
>
> **— Robert Heller**

POINTS TO REMEMBER

DEMOTIVATORS: DUE TO INAPPROPRIATE LEADERSHIP STYLE

- A false promise may motivate an individual momentarily. The moment he realizes that he is being cheated, his enthusiasm evaporates and brings him to a standstill.
- One can retain an individual physically, not mentally. The day an individual comes to know that he is being retained just because he is producing good results, his enthusiasm drains. A feeling of being cheated develops, which stops him from putting efforts that were producing extraordinary results.
- Human beings desire friendly and close interpersonal relationships. They have a desire to be liked and accepted. They strive for friendship, prefer cooperative situations rather than competitive ones, and desire relationships involving a high degree of mutual understanding.
- Conflicting behaviours of superiors creates dissatisfaction among other team members. In the end the team members lose faith in the system and the superiors.
- The feeling of favouritism demotivates team members.
- Comparing two individuals affects the self-esteem of the one who is found inferior. He loses not only the respect in the eyes of others, but also his own self-respect.
- A denial of request for leave comes as a sudden block to the individual's pleasant thoughts, which leads to distaste. Once the leave is refused, an individual may be physically present at work but mentally absent.
- Asking people to work on Sundays/holidays or put extra hours leads to the dissatisfaction. If it is a routine, it frustrates people, and eventually demotivates them.
- Giving undue acknowledgement or appreciation to an individual's contribution may not necessarily produce desired results as it may cause dissatisfaction among others. A persistent feeling of dissatisfaction demotivates other team members.
- One should never ask team members to do something that one wouldn't like to do oneself. ▶

- People expect seniors to be willing to help them.
- Ridiculing not only demotivates an individual in carrying out the present job, but also affects his future endeavours.
- Reprimanding in front of others often leads to demotivation, with the employee losing self-respect, and respect in the eyes of others.
- Motivation means getting somebody to do something because the individual wanted to do it.
- The individual who wants to make a career in an organization, if not recognized, loses hope of being rewarded. He may get demotivated and leave the organization.
- Success of the team depends upon the results of the achievers as well as those of the mediocres and laggards.
- If one often gives negative suggestions or instructions to team members, he makes them inhibited and over a period of time makes them lose their confidence.
- Negative opinion of others contributes to a negative self-image and leads to loss of confidence and morale, ultimately leading to demotivation.
- Instead of adding new procedures one should try to find out the merits in the old procedures. Instead of changing procedures completely, it is better to bring modifications in the existing ones that may deliver better results.
- Delegation helps team members develop their skills and gain experience. No doubt, control is an integral part of delegation. However, questioning every now and then not only irritates team members, but also gives them an impression that their seniors do not have confidence in them. In the long run, it leaves them with a feeling of dissatisfaction.

DEMOTIVATORS: CRITICISM

As a senior it is your duty to appraise your team member on his activities, performance or a proposal submitted by him. Howsoever gentle or factual the criticism is, it does hurt people. There is an old Hindi saying:

Nindak niyare rakhiye, angan kuti chavaye.
Bin sabun pani bina nirmal kare suabhaye.

This means we must keep a critic close to us, which will clean us without soap and water. However, the fact is no one likes to be criticized either by oneself or by others. Most of the time criticism creates sour feelings about the critic. If people develop sour feelings every time you criticize them, this will certainly lead to demotivation.

1. 'Criticizing', an Art

In order to ensure that your criticism is not only heard, but also accepted in the right spirit by your team members, you need to establish your credibility and genuineness. Once they know that this person's objective is to guide me and not to pull my leg, they will be willing to listen to your criticism. Once they listen and accept, they will start implementing your suggestions. This will be an assurance to you that they are taking your criticism in the right spirit.

> **"Every criticism should be made into a sandwich with the bread of praise on the either side."**
>
> **— Unknown**

2. Criticize the Act and Not the Person

Unfortunately, most of the managers do not convey their criticism until they become angry with the person. In their anger when they start expressing criticism, they hurt the person rather than help him. Remember, your objective is to inform people about their shortcomings and not to hurt them. Therefore, while criticizing people you must keep in mind that you are criticizing the act and not the person. You should criticize the person as if you are talking to your friend. The moment they will realize their fault they will become more receptive and will implement your suggestions gladly.

3. Let People Introspect

It is true, that people do not change until they themselves want to change. Hence, you should encourage team members to analyse their own selves. You should try to inculcate the habit of self-evaluation in them. Until they realize the areas of their improvement, they cannot bring a change in themselves. Instead of criticizing them you should ask them to introspect. Once they have analysed their performance, you should give your observations. At the outset, you must mention the points where you would like to appreciate them and then state the area of improvement.

4. Don't Label the Person as a Regular Defaulter

Another point, which you must keep in your mind: never label a person. For example, "You are *always* late." When you say this, you are labelling the person as a regular defaulter. It could be that a person comes late most of the time. However, instead of criticizing the person you must analyse what you did when he came late for the first time. You probably ignored it because you never wanted to upset him. Was it that you were afraid that making him unhappy would lead to diminished results? These are all myths which people have developed. In reality, it works otherwise. Even a child expects parents to point out or reprimand if he commits a mistake. If you had pointed out to him when he came late the first time, he might not have repeated the same act.

5. Use Peer Pressure

An important point which you must keep in mind while offering constructive criticism is that sometimes people resist accepting your suggestions as they consider it difficult to implement. They will have a feeling that it might not be difficult for you since you are an experienced person, but it may not be possible for them. However, if the same suggestion is given by one of their colleagues this feeling will not arise. It is observed that children often learn more quickly from elder brothers and sisters than they do from their parents. The same is true for your team members as well. Especially while pointing out a common area of improvement, you must take the help of a team member who is positive. If he is convinced with your argument or suggestion he will be able to convince the other team members better, as he is a part of them. This does not mean that your acceptance may not be as good as their own peers. However, it is true that people find criticism easier to accept from those whom they find exactly like them.

6. Be Patient

Last but not the least, you must be patient with people. Once you have offered your criticism, give them some time to improve. Nevertheless, you must not miss an opportunity to compliment or reward on even the slightest evidence that they are trying to improve.

> **"Appreciation can make a day. Even change a life. Your willingness to put it into words is all that is necessary".**
>
> **— Margaret Cousins**

GOLDEN RULE OF MANAGEMENT

Follow the golden rule of managing people, "Praise in public and criticize in private." Give credit in public for a job well done. However, criticize or reprimand in private. While being critical, explain what he should do to improve or not repeat the same mistake. The objective of criticizing is to bring back the person to work and not to demotivate and take him away from putting his heart into the work.

For a critical conversation, you need privacy. Well, this meeting need not be in a hotel room or office. It can be held even outside the office, in the customer's chamber or shop or while travelling. The only criterion is nobody other than the two of you should listen to the conversation.

Remember, your team member knows that he has committed a mistake. If you start criticizing him, he would justify his actions. On the contrary, if you explain in private, his guard will be lowered and he will listen to your comments and suggestion carefully and would implement them with enthusiasm.

Gurmeet was a dedicated, sincere representative with seven years of experience in the field. He was one of the best performers. His new Frontline Manager Jayant came to his territory and in the very first visit, this interesting incident occurred. Both of them had just finished the first call; before Jayant could analyse the call, Gurmeet took him to the second customer. Jayant wanted to analyse the first call before making the second call. Hence, while waiting for the next call, Jayant started discussing the first call. Jayant found Gurmeet's approach quite indifferent, as he did not respond properly to most of his questions. They finished the second call and as per usual practice. Jayant wanted to analyse the call before they proceeded to the next call. The moment Jayant asked his opinion about the call they had just made, Gurmeet very candidly told him, "Sir, in case you want to do this analysis, please do it in the evening in your hotel room and not here." His response amazed Jayant, hence he replied, "Well by evening I may not exactly remember all the points hence, I would like to have these discussions after each call."

On his insistence, Gurmeet told him the reason for his reluctance to do it immediately. He said, "Did you notice, while you were analysing the call who was standing behind us? There was an attendant and a junior representative of some other company." Jayant could now realize the reason for his indifferent behaviour during the discussions. It was not that Gurmeet was reluctant to discuss his areas of improvement, but he never wanted it in front of anybody else. Jayant apologized for the same but asked him that immediately after each call he should decide a place where nobody other than two of them are present. Though Jayant's intentions were positive, Gurmeet perceived them negatively since the place was not conducive for criticism.

✔ POINTS TO REMEMBER

DEMOTIVATORS: CRITICISM

- Criticism may create sour feelings about the critic. If people develop sour feelings every time one criticizes them, it will certainly lead to demotivation.
- Once people know that the objective of criticism is to guide and not to pull their leg, they will be willing to listen to the criticism readily.
- In anger, criticism hurts the person rather than helping him. Remember, the objective of criticism is to inform people about their shortcomings and not hurt them.
- One must criticize the act and not the person.
- Instead of criticizing one must ask people to introspect. Once people analyse their own performance, they themselves get the clues to improve their performance.
- While offering suggestions one must mention the positive points first and then the areas of improvement.
- Never label a person as a regular defaulter.
- Howsoever constructive a criticism it may be, people resist accepting suggestions of seniors. The same suggestion, if given by one of their colleagues, is accepted more readily.
- One must not miss an opportunity to compliment or reward people.
- Praise in public and criticize in private. Give credit for a job well done in front of others; criticize or reprimand in private.

DEMOTIVATORS: INAPPROPRIATE COMMUNICATION

Communication is not as easy as we think. Effective communication is to get your message understood by the others so that the exchange of messages moves forward, that too in the direction in which you want it to. However, most of us while communicating forget this fundamental principle.

You may choose appropriate words but what is the guarantee that your communication will leave the desired impact on your team member? Remember, there are two parts to verbal communication, i.e. linguistic and para-linguistic. The words that you speak are known as linguistic component of communication, whereas how you deliver those words, i.e. tone, voice modulation, accent and mannerism account for the para-linguistic component. Your success of verbal communication depends on your ability to strike the right balance between the two. Your tone of voice alone can change the meaning of your message. For example, when you are angry or happy with someone, it is your tone of voice which communicates your feelings to the receiver. The wrong tone may prove to be counterproductive.

It is observed that managers start shouting at their team members even for a simple mistake. Shouting not only affects the team member's self-esteem but also stops seniors from communicating. If it is done often, it puts off people from listening to the speaker. People become apprehensive and stop going to a senior who always shouts. This restricts even their normal efforts. Ultimately their withdrawal frustrates them and leads to their cause of demotivation.

> **"Human beings are the most fragile commodity; they get shattered with just a word."**

Hence, while communicating you must be watchful and work upon improving your ability to use an appropriate tone. Seriousness of your message can be communicated easily by using the appropriate tone rather than shouting. Shouting only creates sour feelings. Selection of words is equally important.

> **"Words are like bullets of a gun. If used improperly, they hurt a person permanently; scars remain for a lifetime".**
>
> **— Unknown**

Improper Body Language

In face-to-face communication, apart from linguistic and para-linguistic aspects there is yet another aspect that accounts for its effectiveness, i.e. non-verbal component. There is a wide range of unconscious physical movements which go with face-to-face communication. These movements can either strengthen or spoil communication. These movements include gestures, postures, facial expressions, eye contact, etc. These non-verbal movements create impacts that help you to convey your emotions, attitudes, feelings and thoughts clearly.

Remember, words alone can't express the inner feelings of a person or the continuing conflicts in his mind or his attitude. As long as your words and body language are consistent, your team members believe in you. The moment your words and body language communicate different things, i.e. facial expression differs from your words, they may have a doubt about your spoken words. If it happens often, they may lose faith in you. Your gestures reinforce your words and ideas. Among all other physical movements, which go along with your communication, facial expressions are the most important as your inner feelings are reflected through your face. People may forget your spoken words but remember your facial expressions. Your facial expression should match your spoken words. For example, if you are happy about an act of your team member but while appreciating it your face does not reflect happiness, you may not be able to communicate your feelings.

> **"Tone of voice, look and manner can prove no less eloquent than choice of words."**
>
> **— Francois La Rochefoucauld**

Therefore, you must be aware of your facial expressions while communicating. Watch your facial expressions, while talking to someone on the phone by looking at a mirror. You will come to know how you look like while speaking. If you find yourself making unpleasant facial expressions try to correct them through conscious effort. Practise smiling and looking pleasant while you communicate.

Barriers in Communication

Apart from improving the delivery of the message, you need to pay attention to certain acts that may come as an obstacle while communicating. If your team members encounter these barriers, they will be dissatisfied while communicating with you. Ultimately their dissatisfaction may become a cause of their demotivation.

1. *Not paying attention*

If you do not pay proper attention to what your team member is trying to communicate, you create a barrier. If it is done routinely, your team member may be reluctant to speak to you or totally stop communicating with you.

2. *Preconceived notions about the speaker*

If you have a preconceived notion about your team member, the same will become a barrier to your communication. For example, if you are of the opinion that a particular team member is casual or is not a person whom you can trust, until you change your notion about him, you may not accept whatever he says or does.

3. *Passivity*

If you have a negative thought or feeling about your team member while communicating, this passivity will come as a barrier. Whatever you listen will be camouflaged by negative thoughts.

4. *Selective listening or not listening*

This is one of the most common barriers people face. As a senior you may have different expectations from a team member. However, while your team member comes to you he has his set of assumptions and expectations. When he tries to communicate, instead of giving patient hearing you resort to selective listening or stop listening. This stops him from communicating the right message. In the bargain neither you nor your team member is able to communicate to the other. If it happens quite often, your team members may stop coming to you for solutions. Over a period it may demotivate them.

> "Spend as much time as possible with all levels of staff, and make it clear that you appreciate feedback and are willing to listen and respond."
>
> — Robert Heller

5. ***Aggressive Communication***

If your approach is aggressive, it will serve as a barrier. It is observed that some managers, in their overenthusiasm for communicating an action-plan resort to an aggressive approach. It is good to push people to attain heights. However, little do they realize that their aggression may become a cause of withdrawal of one of their team members. This may inhibit him from producing results which he is capable of.

Similarly, if your team member commits a mistake or fails to deliver and you start firing the person, you may fail to communicate the real message. The real message is realization of the fact by the person himself that he could not deliver. Remember, your objective is to make your team member realize the mistake and not to fire him. Your firing will diminish his self-esteem. If this happens often, it may lead to demotivation. Therefore, you should resort to assertive communication, i.e. communicating your message and feelings without being aggressive.

TIPS FOR IMPROVING VERBAL COMMUNICATION

- The first and the foremost requisite for effective communication is to construct a correct and appropriate message. Once you have constructed the message, you need to test it on the points mentioned above. This will ensure that it will not lead to your team member's dissatisfaction.
- Once the message is constructed, you must plan the best time to communicate it. Your team member might not take a message in its right spirit if the timing is not appropriate. For example, if you have to criticize or reprimand a team member, do not do it first thing in the morning. Do it in the afternoon or evening after both of you have finished most of the day's work and both of you are relatively free. His guard will be lowered and he will be willing to not only listen, but implement your suggestions as well.
- Needless to mention that your ability to articulate your voice and proper modulation, i.e. paralinguistic communication, will help you to communicate messages and feelings appropriately.

✓ TIPS FOR IMPROVING LISTENING SKILLS

- **Always look at the person speaking to you.** This reflects your interest towards the speaker. You must have observed a child insisting on a careful look while he is communicating to his parents. Even a child knows that if his father or mother is not looking at him, he/she is not listening or at least not attentive. Hence, always look into the eye of the person speaking to you.
- **Show interest in what the other person is saying.** Try to empathize with the other person by understanding or following the topic he is communicating. Use encouraging nods or words, e.g. "Oh I see", "yes", "good", "excellent", etc. Even your body language should reflect your interest. You must lean towards the person speaking to you and use other positive body movements. Inappropriate body language will convey your lack of interest in what the person is trying to communicate. This will be counterproductive and may lead to dissatisfaction.
- **Try to discover the meanings.** You must try to find out the reasons behind each statement made by the speaker. This will help you to understand the whole sequence of facts or his thought process. Never interrupt, rather request for more details. You must try to know the exact meaning of the words he is delivering. You must carefully observe his body language while you listen to him.
- **Use the other person's words while answering or responding.** This reflects your interest in what is being communicated and at the same time helps you to correct your understanding. If you are unable to relate in the same manner, as desired by your team member, he will certainly let you know. You may use the following sentences as guidelines:
    - If I have understood you correctly…
    - Do you mean to say that…
    - You seem to feel upset…
    - In other words, your main problem is…

> "The greatest motivational act one person can do for another is to listen."
>
> — Roy E. Moody

WRITTEN COMMUNICATION

The basics of written communication remain the same, i.e. to get your message understood by the reader in the way you want it to. Therefore, whether you are appreciating or reprimanding, seeking explanation or asking for clarification, your communication should be clear.

Whatever the purpose of communication, your letter should be tailormade in such a way that the reader not only understands the message, but also takes necessary actions as desired by you. Your language and selection of words should be appropriate. However, your written memo can be misunderstood because the receiver is not in front of you. Another point which you must keep in your mind is that a written communication, especially for reprimanding or seeking explanation, may leave a permanent scar on your team member's heart. Therefore, until the situation warrants, you should not write such letters. While asking for a clarification you should avoid written communication as your team member may take it as seeking explanation. If the tone of every letter of yours is that of seeking explanation, the team member will not even be interested in going through its contents, leave alone in responding to it.

Hence, in order to get a positive response while communicating in writing to your team member, you must keep in mind how he will react to it. While suggesting an action plan, if you start your letter by informing them about the benefits they will get by implementing your plan, it will create more interest.

TIPS FOR EFFECTIVE WRITTEN COMMUNICATION

- Your write-up should be written in simple language, so that the other person may understand it clearly.
- You must plan every sentence and the sequence of sentences.
- In order to ensure the accuracy of written communication you must reread your letter before posting it. Many a time while rereading, you yourself will identify areas for improvement.
- Rarely, if you are writing an important letter, should you ask someone else to read it. He may be unaware of the topic you have written on. However, if he can understand a part of it, you may take it for granted that the person whom you are writing to will certainly understand the meaning.

POINTS TO REMEMBER

DEMOTIVATORS: INAPPROPRIATE COMMUNICATION

- Effective communication is to get the message understood by others so that the exchange of messages moves forward, that too in the direction in which you want it to.
- The success of verbal communication depends upon the individual's ability to strike the right balance between linguistic as well as para-linguistic aspects.
- Shouting not only affects a team member's self-esteem, but also stops seniors from communicating.
- Words are like bullets; if used improperly, they hurt a person permanently, the scars remain for life.
- Words alone can't express the inner feelings of a person, the continuing conflicts in his mind or his attitude. As long as words and body language are consistent, people believe the words.

Barriers in Communication

- Not paying proper attention to what others are trying to communicate.
- Preconceived notions about others.
- Negative thoughts or feelings about others while communicating.
- Selective listening.
- Using aggressive approach

All the above-mentioned barriers not only put a brake to communication, but may inhibit people from producing results that they are capable of.

Tips for Improving Verbal Communication

- Construct a correct and appropriate message.
- Plan the best time to communicate.
- Ability to articulate and voice proper modulation, i.e. paralinguistic communication, helps to communicate appropriate messages and feelings.

▶

Tips for Improving Listening Skills

- Look into the speaker's eye.
- Show interest in what the other person is saying.
- Use encouraging nods or words like "oh, I see", "yes", "good", "excellent", etc.
- Inappropriate body language conveys lack of interest in what the person is trying to communicate.
- Understand the meaning behind each statement made by the speaker and use the speaker's words while answering or responding. This improves listening.

Tips for Effective Written Communication

- Write-up should be written in simple language so that the other person may understand it clearly.
- Plan every sentence and the sequence of sentences.
- To ensure accuracy, read and reread the letter before posting it. Alternatively, ask someone else to read.

SIGNALS OF MOTIVATIONAL PROBLEMS

Sohan, an extraordinarily brilliant young man got selected in a multi-national FMCG company. He was excited. Ever since he joined management school, it was his dream to join this company. He was offered a handsome package, which, apart from a good salary included a house and a car. He was given a spacious cabin in a newly constructed office. The office cafeteria served food that tasted like it was cooked at home. Within three months of his joining, he got an opportunity to attend a training programme conducted in Singapore, a place he always wanted to visit.

It came as a surprise to everyone when he left the job within six months. What was more shocking was that he did not have a job in hand at the time of resigning.

Can you identify the reason for Sohan leaving the company that he always wanted to work for? It could be one of the reasons mentioned in this chapter or it could simply be the indifferent behaviour of his immediate boss. Whether people stay and thrive in an organization or they quit depends upon their immediate superior. No doubt, money is important. However, beyond a point money doesn't matter. What matters to people is how his superiors treat him and how valuable he is considered for the organization.

Just like Sohan a vast number of talented people leave organizations despite being offered the best salaries in the industry. This is the height of dissatisfaction resulting in demotivation that forces them to take this extreme step. Remember, your team members are free agents and not the fixed assets of your organization. If you become too controlling, too suspicious, too pushy or too critical, it can stress out your team members. If this continues every time they interact with you, they may decide to leave you and not necessarily your organization. Often, it is a seemingly minor issue that may instigate them to quit.

"It isn't the 100th blow that knocks a good man down, it's the 99 that went before."

— Unknown

If one of your team members leaves your team, what would it cost you and your organization? Apart from the cost of finding a suitable replacement and training him, your organization will have to pay the cost for not having someone to do the job that was assigned to him. If the person was dealing with the external environment, the cost will be much more. It will include the loss of customers, the contacts the person had with the industry, and the loss of business secrets this person may now share with others. It will also result in the loss of morale among co-workers and of course, the loss of the company's reputation.

> **"Every person who leaves an organization then becomes its ambassador, for better or for worse."**
>
> **— Unknown**

By now you must have understood how difficult it is to motivate a person, and also how easy it is to demotivate him. Many a time, even an unintentional move can lead to the demotivation of your team member. Therefore, it is important for you to keep observing the signals your team members may give you when he is getting demotivated. The moment you get any such signal, take corrective steps; otherwise you may lose a good team member forever.

You can expect the following motivational problems when a team member starts giving signals: such as,

- Lack of enthusiasm
- Ignores actions suggested
- Avoids responsibility
- Comes in late, and wants to leave early
- Taking leave, especially on important occasions
- Shows resentment while working with poor tools/equipment
- Stops meeting deadlines
- Displays lack of team spirit
- Wants a break to have fun during working hours
- Doesn't accept any of your special requests
- Magnifies a minor problem into a big one
- Spends too much time on outside activities/interests, such as union activities or running a business of his own
- Anti-management attitude

"Leadership is the ability of a single individual through his or her actions to motivate others to higher levels of achievement."
— F. G. "Buck" Rodgers

How to Motivate

People are in general motivated. They want to work hard and enjoy their life. They want to give their best and be recognized. However, as discussed in the previous chapter, there are circumstances that take away the pleasure of working and make employees dissatisfied. Hence, whenever you are confronted with feelings such as:

- "Why do I always get bad people (colleagues and superiors) to work with?"
- "Why doesn't he obey my instructions?"
- "I have never met such an ungrateful person."
- "I love my people. Why does this colleague hate me?"
- "This person just wants to embarrass me."

instead of reacting and taking action in haste, ponder for a while. These feelings signify your point of view. Are you aware of others' viewpoint? This lack of understanding of others keeps them away from offering you their best. Hence, let us find out what really makes people feel happy and satisfied. Majority of people want that

- They should be assigned an interesting job.
- The job should have an element of stretch that poses a challenge to their capabilities.
- They should be informed clearly what is expected from them.
- They should be able to measure their progress periodically.
- They need to be recognized for the jobs accomplished well.
- They should be provided opportunities for the development of knowledge and skills.
- They need to be respected (both by colleagues and seniors).
- They should be given a patient listening, while they explain their hardships.

- They should know what is there in it (benefits) for them.
- They should have a competent leader to work under.

Now that you know what makes your team members feel happy and satisfied, let us do some exercises. These exercises will help you ascertain to what extent you are able to make your team members feel happy and satisfied. In addition, it will help you get feedback for your own development.

Exercise 1

Do you provide opportunities that make your team members feel happy and satisfied?

Please rate yourself on a scale of 1 to 5
- **5 means: always**
- **4 means: most of the time**
- **3 means: sometimes**
- **2 means: rarely**
- **1 means: never**

1. I assign jobs to my team members, keeping in mind their interest towards the job. ___
2. I add an element of stretch in their goal that may pose a challenge to their capabilities. ___
3. I clearly inform them what is expected from them. ___
4. I periodically provide them feedback on their progress. ___
5. I recognize my team members even on small but well-accomplished jobs. ___
6. I provide opportunities to my team members for their development of knowledge and skills. ___
7. I respect each of my team members. ___
8. I give my team members a patient listening when they explain their hardships. ___
9. I make sure that each of my team member knows what benefits they will be able to derive. ___
10. I regularly update my own knowledge and skill base to remain competent. ___
11. I am interested in my team members' development, and I value their ideas for problem solving. ___
12. I provide opportunities to my team members to develop their competencies. ___
13. I treat all my team members alike. ___
14. I share my plans, goals and objectives with my team members. ___
15. I encourage my team members to think creatively and innovate better methods to do the job. ___

Exercise 2

How do I feel working with my team leader?

> **Please rate yourself on a scale of 1 to 5**
> - **5 means: always**
> - **4 means: most of the time**
> - **3 means: sometimes**
> - **2 means: rarely**
> - **1 means: never**

1. My team leader assigns jobs to me, keeping in mind my interest towards the job. ___
2. My team leader adds an element of stretch in my goal that poses a challenge to my capabilities. ___
3. My team leader while assigning a job clearly informs me what he expects from me. ___
4. My team leader provides me periodical feedback on my progress. ___
5. My team leader recognizes my efforts even on the small jobs that I accomplished well. ___
6. My team leader provides opportunities for the development of knowledge and skills. ___
7. My team leader respects me. ___
8. My team leader gives me a patient listening when I explain the hardships I face. ___
9. My team leader makes sure that I know what benefits I will be able to derive. ___
10. My team leader regularly updates his knowledge and skill base and is competent. ___
11. My team leader is interested in my development and values my ideas for problem solving. ___
12. My team leader provides me opportunities to develop my competencies. ___
13. My team leader treats all my team members alike. ___
14. My team leader shares his plans, goals and objectives with me. ___
15. My team leader encourages me to think creatively and innovate better methods to do the job. ___

Scoring Key

- **A score of 61 to 75 means you are an outstanding leader.**
- **A score of 46 to 60 means you have the potential to be a good leader, you need a little more practice.**
- **A score of 31 to 45 means despite your efforts, you are unable to provide opportunities to your team members to be happy and satisfied.**
- **A score of 15 to 30 means you are unfit to be a leader, hence get out of the way of your team members' success.**

The first exercise will provide you an opportunity to introspect and visualize how often you provide opportunities that make your team members feel happy and satisfied. The answer will be based upon your own observations as well as judgement. However, this signifies only your opinion about yourself. Do your team members also consider you a good leader? To answer this, please ask your team members to do the second exercise. Scoring for both the first and the second exercise remains the same. Once your team members complete the exercise, take out the average marks given by them to you under each head.

Now you have the marks given by you and your team members under each head. Reading these marks in isolation may not be of much use. To get a meaningful feedback on your leadership, you must plot both the marks on a same sheet of paper under each head. Any dissonance in both the marks will be apparent and that is the area for your improvement. For example, your answer to question no. 10 is a perfect 5, whereas, the average score given by your team members to the same question is 3 or 4. Then there is a dissonance. This will force you to once again introspect and find out the areas where you still need to improve as far as your on-the-job competency is concerned.

Remember, "You *cannot* motivate anybody." What best you can do is to create the environment, wherein the team members instead of getting demotivated try to motivate themselves. Certainly, human beings are capable of achieving remarkable feats and surpassing their own previous performances, provided they get the right environment and leadership.

Therefore, what can one do to create the right environment? Well, to create the right environment, the first and foremost requirement is to assess the needs and wants of each of your team members.

> **"It would seem that every human being comes at birth into society not as a lump of clay to be moulded by society, but rather as a structure which society may warp or suppress or build upon."**
> **— Abraham Maslow**

Assessing the Needs and Wants of Your Team Members

To motivate your team members you must be aware of their needs and wants. These needs and wants are different for different people and are different at different stages of their career. We have already discussed: a new recruit may appreciate good salary and perquisites, recognition of good work and free time to enjoy personal life. On the contrary, an experienced person may prefer security of job, status within the team, extra responsibilities, promotion, etc. Once you have an idea about an individual's needs and wants, you can plan specific actions for getting the best out of him.

A word of caution:

While assessing, don't be prejudiced and defeat the very purpose. Your focus should be on performance and not on personality or physical appearance. Favouritism and prejudice are counterproductive in motivating a person.

POINTS TO REMEMBER

HOW TO MOTIVATE

- People are in general motivated. They want to work hard and enjoy their lives, and want to give their best and be recognized.
- To motivate team members one must be aware of their needs and wants. These needs and wants are different with different people and are different at different stages of their career.
- While assessing people, don't be prejudiced as it defeats the very purpose. The focus should be on performance and not on personality or physical appearance.
- Favouritism and prejudice are counterproductive in motivating a person.
- Lack of understanding of others keeps them away from offering their best. Remember, people want that:
  - They should be assigned an interesting job.
  - The job should have an element of stretch that poses a challenge to their capabilities.
  - They should be informed clearly what is expected from them.
  - They should be able to measure their progress periodically.
  - They need to be recognized for the jobs accomplished well.
  - They should be provided opportunities for the development of knowledge and skills.
  - They need to be respected (both by their colleagues and seniors).
  - They should be given a patient listening while they explain their hardships.
  - They should know what is there in it (benefits) for them.
  - They should have a competent leader to work for.

DIFFERENT STROKES FOR DIFFERENT FOLKS (PART I)

Society consists of different people, young, adult and old. They are not just different in their age, but their ways of thinking are also radically different from each other. Your team may not be an exception. In a typical workforce there are 'old-timers' (they are not only old in age but also in their way of thinking), 'contemporaries' (not very old but have put in sufficient period in a job) and the 'Generation Next' (just out of college, bubbling with enthusiasm, highly energetic, impatient, eager to change the world).

Gone are those days when managers wanted every employee to experience what they experienced in the early days of their career – autocratic leadership, long working hours and no opportunity to raise their viewpoint. Everybody was managed in the same fashion. However, today in order to motivate each of them you need to adopt different approaches. As discussed earlier, you need to have "different strokes for different folks".

> **"The art of choosing men is not nearly so difficult as the art of enabling those one has chosen to attain their full worth."**
> **— Napoleon Bonaparte**

Old-Timers

In a typical workforce an old-timer may not have independent initiative, yet if you assign a task to him, it will be completed on time. You give old-timers a chance to prove themselves and they will prove their worth. You must respect and reward their work ethics/hard work.

They are motivated by:

- Public recognition.
- While dealing with them a personal touch will fetch better results, e.g. "I want you to do this for me."
- Instead of sending a typed letter, a handwritten note will do a better job.
- Old-timers believe in participative management; you must involve them in discussions/decision making.

- Assist them in gaining name/recognition throughout the company. The photograph with seniors or an important person in the organization is likely to find a place in their home.
- Old-timers are not used to e-mails and faxes. Instead of asking them to communicate through these methods, a post/courier will be better.

> **"Managers help people to see themselves as they are. Leaders help people to see themselves better than they are."**
>
> **— Jim Rohn**

Contemporaries

Contemporaries are generally responsive and have sufficient knowledge as well as understanding of the job. Majority of them are involved in their jobs. Since they might be of your age, they share the same feelings as you do. Hence, before assigning them any task, ask yourself if you were them, how would you take it or react to it.

- Contemporaries may cherish job satisfaction more than any other reward. A little freedom goes a long way to keep them satisfied. You must delegate them the job and offer control; they will work on their own and deliver better results.
- Contemporaries take constructive feedback in the right spirit. They not only improve in the areas suggested to them, but also look forward to feedback in the future.
- Talk to contemporaries about their areas of interest. Take interest in them, their family matters (of course with their consent), their hobbies and liking and they will be ready to die for you.

GENERATION NEXT

In contrast to old-timers or contemporaries, Generation Next has survival mentality. They share feelings such as "It is useless to work for any one company" or "Long hours at work does not necessarily pay off." They like a casual and comfortable atmosphere at work. In order to motivate them you need to understand their mentality and give them plenty of freedom and responsibilities.

- Generation Next enjoys multiple tasks. Assign them projects they can fit in. However, let them prioritize in their own way, they will deliver you results.
- You need to plan plenty of time for their orientation towards the job. Create a clear picture of the work environment in your company, your expectations from them and company's long-term goals, etc.
- You need to learn about their personal goals as well. Develop a strategy for aligning their personal goals with that of your team/ company goals.
- You should expect all sorts of conflicts when you have more than one Generation Next in your team. Be sensitive to their individual needs/ priorities, while trying to resolve the conflicts.
- Generation Next wants to continue their education and develop their skills. You must try to offer opportunities to them.
- Generation Next is familiar with computers and internet. Instead of asking them to send a report by post or courier, email would be better.

DIFFERENT STROKES FOR DIFFERENT FOLKS (PART II)

The great visionary and a very successful leader who transformed himself from an ordinary person to the king-maker of Magadh, Acharya Vishnugupta (Chanakya), classified people into five types:

- *Pradiptapragya* means those who are sharp and dashing
- *Guptapragya* means those who have undiscovered talent
- *Suptapragya* means those who are talented but take no action
- *Truptapragya* means those who are contented
- *Luptapragya* means those who have lost interest

According to Chanakya, while dealing with people, one must identify which type the person belongs to and find out the reasons responsible for his state of mind. Then decide on the action to deal with him.

PRADIPTAPRAGYA

These are the people who are highly motivated. Most of them are self-motivated. Their source of motivation is their belief in their own values. They are sharp and dashing.

Some attributes of *Pradiptapragya*:

- Appealing personality; spend time on their grooming
- Intelligent; have good common sense
- Witty; use presence of mind well
- Energetic; bubbling with enthusiasm
- Eager to perform; love challenges

- Thoughtful; consider various options before action
- Cooperative; eager to help others
- Trusting; can be relied upon
- Receptive; listens to suggestions of others

To keep a *Pradiptapragya* motivated is like adding fuel to fire. Keep adding fuel to their fire.

These people can be motivated by

- Offering challenging jobs
- Listening carefully to their suggestions
- Inviting them to help others
- Entrusting greater responsibilities
- Asking their suggestions to solve problems

GUPTAPRAGYA

A *Guptapragya* is like a mango or a rubber tree in its budding stage. These trees take a few years to grow before giving fruits or rubber. But, farmers patiently nurture these plants. They know that once these saplings become trees, the returns will be enormous. Similarly, *Guptapragyas* in your team are the people you need to invest your managerial input in. Once they develop themselves, they will pay you back whatever investment you have made on their development. They have undiscovered talent.

Some attributes of *Guptapragya*:

- Modest
- Shy in nature
- Slow to act
- Apprehensive
- Introvert

Therefore, you need to persuade a *Guptapragya* to accept a challenging task. Once he accepts it, you need not explain or demonstrate; just a word of encouragement will do the rest.

These people can be motivated by:

- Persuading to accept challenging jobs
- Demonstrating difficult tasks
- Encouraging to take independent decisions
- Encouraging to mix with people/team members
- Allowing them to speak in public (during meetings)

I am sure you have read in the *Ramayana* the episode of Hanumanji crossing the sea to reach Lanka. Until the time Jambuvantji persuaded him by saying these words, "*Kavan so kaj kathin jag manhi, jo nahi hot tat tum panhi?*" (Which is that difficult task in the world that you cannot do?) Even Hanumanji did not believe that he could cross the sea.

SUPTAPRAGYA

Suptapragya are the people who by nature are talented but take no action.

Some attributes of *Suptapragya*:

- Introvert
- Lethargic
- Slow in action
- Lacking enthusiasm
- Over-critical

These people live their lives like somnambulists, or those who walk while sleeping. However, unlike a patient of somnabulism, they are cognizant. They know a minimum amount of effort is needed to sustain their jobs. Hence, they always limit their potential. Until these people are awakened from their sleep, they will not produce the desired results.

These people can be motivated by:

- Persuading to take action
- Giving clear-cut but simple suggestions
- Reminding them of their past achievements
- Providing regular feedback on their performance

TRUPTAPRAGYA

Unlike a *Pradiptapragya*, a *Truptapragya* is complacent. Complacency and motivation do not go hand in hand. Rather, both act in opposite directions. Complacency makes people idle; they lose interest in their job. Even to put minimum effort required to carry out their job becomes tedious for them. No wonder these people are contented or complacent.

Some attributes of *Truptapragya*:

- Mature by nature
- Methodical
- Somewhat reserved
- Wants to be in comfort zone, as they lack zeal
- Late in action

To bring back these people into the mainstream is like bringing a lost ship to the shore or to the right path. You need to help them, bring back once again their desire to succeed. Let them experience a little pride, enjoyment and excitement in whatever they do.

These people can be motivated by:

- Involving them in decision making
- Explaining the hidden benefits of a particular action
- Giving importance to them during meetings/interactions
- Persuading them to take decisions/actions by themselves
- Encouraging them to accept higher responsibilities

LUPTAPRAGYA

These are the people who have lost interest.

Some attributes of *Luptapragya*:

- Lack of enthusiasm
- Dull
- Delayed action
- Negative approach towards life or work
- Avoid confrontation/ interactions

These people are very difficult to motivate; however, one must try to find out the exact reason of their loss of interest and accordingly a suitable action should be taken to bring them back to normal state.

Now, the question is do you know who is a *Suptapragya* and a *Luptapragya* in your team? In other words, who is getting demotivated in your team and why? Your approach should be tailored to their individual needs.

Nevertheless, there will be a member who despite all your efforts will do or keeps doing things not expected of him. What to do with him or how do you change his behaviour?

POINTS TO REMEMBER

DIFFERENT STROKES FOR DIFFERENT FOLKS

- In order to motivate different people one needs to adopt different approaches, i.e. "different strokes for different folks".
- An old-timer may not have independent initiative, yet if assigned a task, he completes it on time. One must give old-timers a chance to prove themselves and they will prove their worth.
- Contemporaries are generally responsive, have sufficient knowledge as well as understanding of the job. Before assigning them any task, one must ponder how they would take it or react to it.
- Generation Next likes to have a casual and comfortable atmosphere at work. In order to motivate them one needs to understand their mentality and give them freedom and responsibilities.
- *Pradiptapragya* are highly motivated; most of them are self-motivated. Their source of motivation is their belief in their own values. They are sharp and dashing.
- *Guptapragya* are the people who need investment of managerial input. Once they develop themselves, they will pay back whatever investment is made in their development. They have undiscovered talent.
- *Suptapragya* are the people, who by nature are talented but take no action. They know that a minimum amount of effort is needed to sustain their job. Until these people are awaken from their sleep, they do not produce desired results.
- *Truptapragya* are complacent, that makes them contented.
- *Luptapragya* are the people who have lost interest. One must try to find out the exact reason for their loss of interest, and accordingly a suitable action should be taken to bring them back to normal.
- Success depends upon individual's ability to identify who is a *Suptapragya* and for that matter a *Luptapragya*.

BEHAVIOUR MODIFICATION

The behaviour of a person reflects his inner self, i.e., attitude. An individual acquires attitudes from parents, teachers, family members, friends, peers, and society at large. In the early years, one forms attitudes by imitating others, especially those whom one admires, respects, or even fears and who become role models. Over a period the actions that an individual imitates become his own and he develops perceptions based on what the role models considered right or wrong. These perceptions lead to a set mode of thinking based on one's own actions or experiences. This mindset is responsible for the individual's actions in any given situation.

> **"The behaviour of a person is a reflection of his inner self, i.e. attitude."**
>
> **— Unknown**

Perception

Perceptions of an individual cannot be changed as these are based on his childhood experiences. Does this mean that you can do nothing to change the behaviour of your team members? Certainly you can make an attempt. You can make the person learn the expected behaviour or response that will determine his level of:

- Job satisfaction
- Job involvement
- Commitment to the organization

Job Satisfaction: A person with a positive attitude towards his job gets a high level of job satisfaction, and the contrary is also true.

Job Involvement: Job involvement is the degree to which an individual psychologically identifies with his job and considers performance as a tool to prove his self-worth.

Commitment to the Organization: Organizational commitment or loyalty to the organization is a state of mind when the individual identifies an organization's goals with those of his own and continues to work with the organization.

> **"A good objective of leadership is to help those who are doing poorly to do well and to help those who are doing well to do even better."**
>
> **— Jim Rohn**

Attitude

What should you do to change your team member's attitude towards his job and consequently change his behaviour? A change in behaviour occurs because of experiences that result from a particular behaviour. Therefore, you can try to change his perception by changing your behaviour towards him. You can do this, provided you remember what contributed to develop such perceptions in childhood. Have you noticed how a child responds to his parents' behaviour? If he knows that a particular act pleases the parent, he repeats the same to get a kiss or a hug. On the contrary, if an act leads to a slap, the child will not do it or at least will make sure that the parents do not notice it.

> **"You get more of the behaviour you reward. You do not get what you hope for, ask for, wish for or beg for. You get what you reward."**
>
> **— Michael le Boeuf**

Behaviour Depends upon Consequences

If you respond to the behaviour of your team members appropriately, you can certainly force them to change their behaviour. If the consequence of a behaviour is:

Pleasant or desirable:	Behaviour is reinforced and often repeated.
Unpleasant or undesirable:	Behaviour is not likely to be repeated.

To mould your team members according to your or your organization's expectations, you need to adopt a systematic approach, known as 'behaviour shaping'.

POINTS TO REMEMBER

BEHAVIOUR MODIFICATION

- The behaviour of a person reflects his inner self, i.e. attitude, which is responsible for the individual's actions/behaviour in any given situation.
- A person with positive attitude towards his job gets a high level of job satisfaction, and the contrary is also true.
- The degree to which an individual psychologically identifies with his job and considers performance as a tool to prove his self-worth determines his involvement in the job.
- Organizational commitment or loyalty to the organization is a state of mind that makes people continue to work with the same organization.
- Change in the behaviour of an individual occurs because of experiences that result from a particular behaviour.
- If the consequence of a behaviour is pleasant or desirable, the behaviour is reinforced and often repeated, whereas if it is unpleasant or undesirable, the behaviour is not likely to be repeated.

BEHAVIOUR SHAPING

Shaping human behaviour is similar to that of shaping an earthen pot. Have you ever observed a potter giving shape to an earthen pot, especially a big pot like a flower vase? While giving the shape of a pot to a lump of clay, the potter uses different strokes. Giving the initial shape of a round pot, he gently holds the pot so that it does not fall, and strokes it gently to give it a proper shape. Similarly, you need to shape the behaviour of your team members by giving different strokes.

METHODS OF BEHAVIOUR SHAPING

You can shape the behaviour of your team members in five ways:

- Positive reinforcement
- Negative reinforcement
- Punishment
- Sedated positive stroke
- Extinction

Positive Reinforcement

If the consequence of a behaviour is pleasant or desirable, the behaviour gets reinforced and is often repeated. Every time your team member does something right, praise him. Your praise reinforces permanent positive learning. Praise is the most powerful tool a manager has in his armamentarium.

> **"Catch the person doing the right thing. Fail to reward the right behaviour and be ready for the wrong result."**
>
> **— Unknown**

There are various ways to offer positive reinforcement, for example a pat on the back or wishing a person by saying, "Congratulations" or "Congrats, you did it", etc. If your team member is posted to some other place, you may write a letter of appreciation for the job done well. If a team member excels, a few lines of appreciation will work as positive reinforcement. You can highlight the appreciation further. Instead of a personal letter, send a circular addressed to all your team members saying, "Let us all together congratulate Mr. X for ...."

✓ TIPS FOR OFFERING POSITIVE REINFORCEMENT

Remember, words alone do not necessarily communicate your feelings; it is the paralinguistic and the non-verbal clues that help you to pass on your message correctly. Therefore, while offering a positive reinforcement you must keep in mind all the three important attributes of an ideal praise, i.e. essence, approach and body language.

Essence: You must phrase your words in such a way that it communicates the gist of your praise quickly but explicitly and specifically for the job done well.

Approach: You must focus on voice modulation so as it gives the required shade to your message. For example, if you praise somebody on an excellent performance but the tone of your voice is flat, it will not help you communicate your feelings. Similarly, if your tone is not appropriate, even though you are praising, the person will get a different message.

Body Language: You must also watch your body language. If your words are not consistent with the non-verbal signals, you will fail to deliver the message. In addition, it will communicate that you are not sincere. Hence, while appreciating or communicating the good news you must look straight into the eyes of your team member. A smile will go a long way to leave an ever-lasting impact on your team member.

Negative Reinforcement

If the consequence of a behaviour is unpleasant or undesirable, that behaviour is not likely to be repeated. You must have observed that children keep looking at their parents while doing a mischievous act. If the parents' response to their act is positive or somewhat indifferent they keep doing the act. However, if the response is negative, they immediately stop it. Unfortunately, these childhood reflexes do not go away as life advances, for even as adults human beings look for reinforcements to decide their course of action. Therefore, in order to stop a person from doing an undesirable act you need to offer negative reinforcement. For example, a particular team member does not comply with the instructions given to him or does not send his reports in time. A letter informing or reminding him about the deadline for reporting or instructing him to send the report or to take the desired action within the stipulated time will work as a negative reinforcement.

Every time a person fails to meet a deadline, he should be reminded that he failed to comply. You may send a reminder/note/memo. More than just reminding or penalizing, the tone of your communication should be to make people aware that their activities are monitored.

Punishment

Punishment is both complicated and troublesome. However most managers use it very liberally. Punishment should be used only after all your attempts to change the person's behaviour have failed or if you observe the behaviour of a team member is significantly impertinent.

Punishment creates unpleasantness. Take the case about delay in sending reports. Add a line in your letter, "If I do not receive your report latest by X date, your daily allowance will be deducted for the number of days the report is delayed." Alternatively, ask him to stop working and meet you in person, both the statements tantamount to punishment.

Punishment is a double-edged sword, it cuts both ways. For example, it may stop a person from doing what is not expected of him, but it may generate bad feelings about you and strain your relationship with him. He may stop doing what he was doing well in the past. For example, take the case of a member who is very good as far as work is concerned but sends reports very late. If you punish him for the delay in sending reports, he may lose interest in the job, which is not desirable. For such a person a negative reinforcement will be more appropriate than punishment.

Another drawback of punishment is that the next time you want to give it, you need to increase the degree. However, if you use punishment frequently, nothing will work. Often it is observed that despite punishing a person the original problem still persists. A particular team member who wants attention, more power, is fearful, or is mischievous may repeat the act again. Hence, punishment should be given very sparingly and judiciously. It should always be for the particular act but not for the person as a whole. Also, punishment should not lead to diminished self-esteem.

This does not mean that punishment should not be used at all. Punishment of a particular behaviour will work as a message for other team members not to commit the same act.

✔ TIPS FOR USING PUNISHMENT AS AN EFFECTIVE TOOL TO MODIFY BEHAVIOUR OF YOUR TEAM MEMBERS

1. You must clearly define and communicate to your team what is proper and improper work behaviour.
2. Your team members should know beforehand the consequences of a particular undesirable behaviour.
3. Before punishing a person, you must be sure that not only the person but also your other team members understand the reason for the punishment.
4. You must clearly explain to your team member why his behaviour is undesirable.
5. You must suggest the alternative behaviour and ways to change the undesirable behaviour.
6. Punishment should be for a precise, perceptible and performance-related behaviour.
7. Punishment should be appropriate to the act.

8. Punishment should be given immediately after the undesirable behaviour. It decreases the confusion and at the same time increases the effectiveness of the punishment.
9. Punishment for a particular act should be same across your team or organization.
10. Punishment should always be administered in isolation.

Sedated Positive Stroke

This is one of the forms of negative reinforcement. The term has contradictions, i.e., positive and sedated. An otherwise good team member sometimes commits silly mistakes. If you ignore the mistakes, he may presume that the mistakes do not matter. If you reinforce it negatively, it may create unnecessary ill feeling, as he might not have done that mistake intentionally. When you face such situations, approach the way a mother approaches her child. A mother uses sedated positive strokes very effectively. When a child does something wrong, the mother says, "If you continue to do this, I will not speak to you." For a small child it works both as a punishment as well as negative reinforcement.

If one of your good team members commits a silly mistake, use sedated positive strokes. Instead of asking, "Why did you do this?" or "Didn't you know how to do this?", you may say, "This was not expected from you." The first two sentences amount to questioning his ability, but the third sentence conveys something like "Although you do well every day, today you could not do that well."

> **"If you want to be successful, it's just this simple. Know what you are doing, love what you are doing, and believe in what you are doing."**
>
> **— Will Rogers**

Extinction

Extinction means the absence of any type of reinforcement or ignoring small acts that may not affect the performance. This term has probably come from extinguishing fire. Fire needs air, temperature and material that can catch fire easily. In the absence of any of the three, fire cannot sustain itself and will extinguish itself.

A sales representative joined the team of a field manager. He was very weak in English. However, he had all other qualities required for being a successful salesperson. The very first month he achieved his target and sent a report to his senior:

Deer Boss,

Ahmedabad sails for the month of January: Rupis 1,75,000/-

Ashok.

On receiving this report, the boss got furious and wrote a long memo to him explaining the reporting procedure and highlighted the spelling mistakes of the words "Dear, sale and Rupees." The next month he received the following report:

Bos,

Ahmedabad sails for the month of February: Rupis 2,00,000/-

Ashok.

His boss once again became furious and went to his senior with a request to terminate the services of the salesperson. After listening to the full story, the senior asked the team leader to instruct the person to send next month's report directly to him. On receiving the report of March wherein once again he registered a sales growth, the senior manager wrote:

Deer Ashok,

Kip on selling and hell with your spellings.

Bos

You can ignore an insignificant, undesirable behaviour as long as it does not affect the performance. Take the case mentioned above, month after month the salesperson is recording growth. He may not be good in English, but it doesn't matter. As long as he is showing improvement in sales, it is good for both you and the organization. Would you appreciate that he sends his reports written in perfect English but with no improvement in sales month after month?

A word of caution:

Extinction does not suggest ignoring even a small aspect, which can affect the morale of other team members or the organization's image.

To sum up:

- Identify the behaviour that needs modification.
- Use positive reinforcement for inculcating good work habits.
- Use negative reinforcements to restrain the person from doing acts that are not expected.
- Use sedated positive strokes depending upon the person's previous record.
- Use punishment very selectively and judiciously.
- Use extinction to discourage and eliminate insignificant undesirable behaviour.

Whether it is positive or negative reinforcement, the key is to "do it immediately". Delay in reinforcing any behaviour diminishes the effectiveness of reinforcement.

HOW TO HANDLE A DEMOTIVATED TEAM MEMBER

However hard you may try, one of your team members may get demotivated due to a situation beyond your control. Once you come across a situation wherein you find a team member getting demotivated, have a frank talk to understand your colleague's point of view and at the same time explain your stance. Call the person for a separate meeting.

TIPS FOR SUCH MEETINGS ARE

- Conduct at a place where both of you can talk freely without any disturbance.
- Create a cordial and relaxing atmosphere.
- Initiate the discussion with some general comments.
- Instead of referring to the issue yourself, invite him to reflect upon it.
- Once the person accepts your perspective, point out the desired behaviour.

- Depending upon his comments, ask for the causes of the changes.
- Instead of providing a solution, ask him to suggest alternatives.
- When he provides alternatives, offer the required support.
- Once both of you come to a consensus for improving the behaviour, fix an appropriate time frame for behaviour modification.

We have discussed a lot about individual's motivation. However, the success of a manager depends upon a group of individuals, who make his team. Hence, let us understand as to what makes a team feel motivated.

> **"The greater the loyalty of a group towards the group, the greater is the motivation among the members to achieve the goals of the group, and greater the probability that the group will achieve its goals."**
>
> **— Rensis Likert**

✓ POINTS TO REMEMBER

BEHAVIOUR SHAPING

- To shape the behaviour of people one needs different strokes, such as positive or negative reinforcement, punishment, sedated positive strokes or extinction.
- A pat on the back or wishing a person by saying, "Congratulations" or "Congrats, you did it", etc. works as positive reinforcement.
- While offering a positive reinforcement one must keep in mind the three important attributes of an ideal praise, i.e. essence, approach and body language.
- Every time a person fails to meet a deadline, he should be reminded that he failed to comply. It can be done by sending a reminder/note/memo. The tone of the communication should be such as it makes people aware that their activities are monitored.
- Punishment should be used only after all attempts to change the person's behaviour fail or if the behaviour of a person is found significantly impertinent.
- Punishment is a double-edged sword. It may stop a person from doing what is not expected, but it may generate lot of ill feelings and may strain relationships.
- Punishment should be given very sparingly and judiciously. It should always be for the particular act but not for the person as a whole.
- An otherwise good team member sometimes commits silly mistakes. In such a case instead of using negative stroke, one should use sedated positive stroke.
- One must ignore an insignificant, undesirable behaviour of people as long as it does not affect the performance.
- Extinction does not suggest ignoring even a small aspect, which can affect the morale of other team members or the organization's image.
- The key to using different strokes is to "do it immediately." Delay in reinforcing any behaviour diminishes the effectiveness of reinforcement.

MOTIVATING A TEAM

Motivated teams contribute to the overall success of the organization. In a motivated team, all the members work in perfect harmony with each other to produce the desired results. Even though each individual works in a specific department or is assigned a specific job function, all are unified to accomplish the team's overall objectives.

> **"Coming together is a beginning, staying together is progress, and working together is success."**
>
> **— Henry Ford**

Participation Motivates

People are often more motivated by how they are used in a job than by how they are treated. Where people feel they are part of an experiment or part of a project, they show a much higher level of motivation. So create a more motivated individual or group by getting people involved.

Many managers do not share their plans, goals and objectives. To get your plans implemented you need to *sell* your ideas.

> **"Don't just tell them. Get them to embrace your ideas"**
>
> **— Unknown**

Attributes of an Effective Team

In an effective team you can count on its each and every member. Team members believe that as a part of a team, everything that they do or don't do, impacts team performance. Hence, they make sure that no matter whose job it is, it must be done, may it be to just return a telephone call, write a report, attend to a customer or a meeting.

Precision

"To do it right, the first time," is the motto of an effective team. To be precise is a matter of pride for both an individual and a team. This also demonstrates a commitment to uphold the standards of the team and thereby generate team pride.

Initiative

Initiative breeds innovation. However, innovation can only flourish if the team members support other colleagues. Taking the lead is a great risk, yet these risks are greatly reduced in a team where members respect each other, forgive mistakes of colleagues and forego their individual differences.

Punctuality

Another important attribute of an effective team is that every member respects the time of others by turning team priorities into personal priorities. All the team members arrive for meetings on time, share information promptly, communicate concisely and above all always seek information with ease, "if it is a good time to initiate interactions/discussions."

Spirit

To be a part of a team is like being a part of a family, where every team member respects and values the opinions of other members. There is mutual trust among the team members. People value every individual's suggestions, communicate openly, manage differences, share success and welcome ideas even from a new member.

TIPS FOR MOTIVATING A TEAM

To keep the team motivated is the key to success for any manager. Very often we listen to statements like, "Let us build a team", "Let us work as a team" or "It is my team", but do we really understand how an effective team is built?

Here are a few tips for building an effective and motivated team.

Goal

First and foremost prerequisite for building an effective team is to establish a SMART goal. A goal should neither be too optimistic nor too pessimistic. SMART stands for

S: A goal must have an element of 'stretch'. In other words, the objective should be a little more than what can be easily achieved. The stretch will stimulate the team members to involve themselves in the job and evolve creative ideas and alternatives that will lead to success. In addition, a goal must also be 'specific'. Vague actions or activities do not get implemented.

M: A goal should be 'measurable', i.e., tangible and quantifiable.

A: A goal should be achievable and action-oriented.

R: A goal should be 'realistic' and 'relevant'; otherwise the purpose of planning gets defeated.

T: The goal should always be 'time bound'. Have specific time limit for completing all the activities.

ROAD to Success —"Right Observation And Direction"

Once you are able to establish the goal, you must explain its importance to the team or organization as a whole. This will make the members feel committed to accomplish the team goal. Therefore, it is important that each of your team members should clearly understand the goal of the team. You must clearly communicate your expectations from each of your team members. If the goal is clear to them and if they feel that it is in line with their own wants and needs, you will be able to sustain their motivation, else it may diminish gradually.

However, team members must also perceive their contribution as valuable to the organization and to their own careers. Hence, you must visualize what your team members anticipate as recognition for their contributions.

Swami had joined as the branch head of a company manufacturing office automation equipments. He had a staff of 12 persons including two peons. While going through the records he realized that the branch was in a real mess. Business was slipping year after year. Though all the 12 employees were there in the branch since its inception, they never considered themselves as part of the organization. The branch was 800 km away from its head office and for the last two years the position of branch head was lying vacant. Since there was nobody to supervise them, they were working at their own pace without having any clear-cut goals. Swami could clearly see the lack of enthusiasm in each of them.

Within the first week of his joining, Swami called a meeting of all the employees including the two peons. He explained to them the vision and mission statements of the organization. He even showed them the corporate presentation that he brought from the HO to show the customers. He could notice the interest shown by his people. In the end he asked each one of them to write on a piece of paper their goals. He could see the hesitation on their faces, as nobody was clear about his goals. On his insistence everybody gave him something in writing, which they considered their goal. He wrote those goals on one side of the white board and on the other side he wrote the organization's goals. Then he asked each one of them to identify what exactly their individual goals should be.

Once everybody had identified their goals, he explained to them the importance of a 'SMART' goal. He could observe the instant change. He asked them to rewrite their goals having all the elements of a 'SMART' goal. He was surprised to see that each one of them could now write their goals meticulously. Needless to mention, in the first year of his taking over the charge of the branch, it was rated as the best branch in the country.

CHALLENGING TASK

Human beings have a survival mechanism known as fight or flight instinct. Whenever confronted with a challenge, even before we start thinking consciously our body starts preparing for its defence. It could be to either run away from the situation, i.e. flight, or address it upfront, i.e. fight. A challenge leads to a rewarding team experience. There are numerous examples when even a mediocre team responds to a challenge with heroic success. Here challenge itself works as a motivator.

> **"There are no great people in this world, only great challenges, which ordinary people rise to meet."**
>
> **— William Frederick Halsey, Jr.**

However, an additional criterion for a challenge is the level of difficulty. If a challenge is too difficult, perhaps it will be perceived as impossible, and team members may give up even before they start working on it. Nevertheless, the same result may occur if the members perceive the challenge as too easy. Hence, you must try to create excitement among the team members by offering them tasks that are challenging yet not impossible. In order to make them accept a challenging task you need to involve the team members in group activities. You must support your team by providing all the required resources. Most important of all, you must invest your time to discuss the problems of team members, give due attention to their concerns or requests and take interest in the work of the team.

Sunder joined as the regional head, Karnataka, of a leading FMCG company. He had a field force of 30 salespersons and 4 managers apart from the office staff of 6 people. During the first review meeting he could observe the lack of enthusiasm in his team. He found people were defensive and there was resentment in their voices. Obviously, the sales picture was also like that. Nobody had achieved the target during the last three years. The average sale of the region was Rs. 580 lakhs per month.

Next day he called his area managers for a review meeting. While reviewing their sales figures he asked them to write the current sales of each territory and also to write in front of those figures the estimated business potential. Once everybody had completed, he wrote all the figures on the board and totalled them. It came as a surprise to everyone when they saw the total. The estimated business potential of the region was Rs. 1002 lakhs per month. All the area managers started looking at each other. Everyone said, "It is impossible." ▶

"Were you kidding while planning?" Sunder asked. There was silence. Sunder broke the silence, "I am sure while estimating these figures you must have considered all those possible avenues of business, which are not providing any revenues currently. Now let's work to ensure that we tap these avenues," he said. The same month the region achieved sales of Rs. 620 lakhs, second month Rs. 710 lakhs, third month Rs. 840 lakhs and fourth month the magic figure was achieved. The region achieved a sale of Rs. 1010 lakhs.

Growth

We learned that growth is the fundamental necessity of life. Right from birth, growth is the basic instinct of a human being that stimulates overall development. If your team members find their job a source of growth in their competencies, they will feel motivated. Hence, it is your responsibility to help them develop their competencies, which will ultimately lead them to achieve their career goals. If your team members feel that they are moving forward, learning new concepts, adding to their skill base, and stretching their minds, their motivation levels will remain high. This also adds value to the individual and helps them enhance their self-esteem and self-worth.

Accordingly, as a team leader you should look for opportunities that will help you develop the competence of team members by imparting the required knowledge, skill, and capability to address the issues that surface during the implementation of strategies.

In addition, you must be ready to provide necessary help to your team members. Their needs may be technical or human. You need to strike a very fine balance between both types of needs. Your timely assistance will reassure your team members that they have resources, strategies, and support needed to accomplish the set goal. In addition, it will ensure that the team members become competent in the work they perform and at the same time are highly functional in their interpersonal relationships.

Aurobindo is a supervisor in a factory manufacturing auto parts. He has 40 workers in his section. His section is responsible for manufacturing two of the important parts his company is selling maximum.

He is a sincere and dedicated person to his job. He is in his late forties. Most of the workers call him *dada* (in Bangla, *dada* means elder brother), not because he is the boss but because they respect him since he is always with them in the hours of need. It may be a problem of the machine or of their family; he is the first person they contact for necessary support/guidance.

The reason for the respect he commands is his willingness to impart 'on-the-job training' to his teammates. Instead of sitting in his cabin, most of the time he is found with the workers on the shopfloor explaining the intricacies of their jobs. Not only the new but experienced workers too, come to him for suggestions/guidance.

One more quality for which everyone admires him is his ability to spot talent. During the last three years, he had recommended six of his workers for promotion as senior apprentice/supervisors to the different departments. Out of these six workers, one person got promoted as supervisor and was transferred to the packaging department and another to a section responsible for manufacturing the highest selling product of their company.

The Need for Belonging

We had discussed, a basic human need – a sense of belonging. Human beings are known as social animals. They always want to be a part of something, a team or society. This association with others is a necessary part of our completeness. Corporate celebrations and events play a vital role in conveying this feeling of togetherness and brotherhood. People identify themselves as a part of the larger team. This in turn persuades them to work together towards common purpose. How to make these events and celebrations memorable is an art. It needs careful planning as well as execution. You may distribute shirts with your team logo on it, or a memento. You can also plan trophies for the team/teams, which have excelled. To do it there is only one guiding principle "Whatever you do, do it top class!" This sends a loud and clear message down the line, that you expect top quality work from them, and they could also expect the same in return.

However, you can also organize such events on your own for your team. For example, on accomplishing a task well, you can throw a party for all the team members. Instead of calling them to a hotel invite them to your house to make a better impact. It may sometimes be bothersome for both you and your family, however, it will be forgotten because of the overwhelming response of your teammates.

Ram recently joined as depot manager in a leading detergent manufacturing company. He has a staff of 20 employees, including 4 packers and 6 deliverymen. His seniors told him about the differences between his predecessor and the staff members. During the first month of his joining, he could notice the indifferent behaviour of the staff. Nobody gave an ear to his suggestions. He, however, knew the reason. Therefore, instead of reacting or forcing them to follow or listen to his suggestions, he kept quite. Next month was the festival of Holi. He invited all the staff members to his house for a Holi Milan. Out of a total staff of 20 people, only 9 came. These people included 3 packers and 4 deliverymen.

He and his wife welcomed them and served the food that was prepared by his wife at home. Since they had prepared the food for 20 people, the next day Ram carried sweets to the office. He personally went to everyone's seat and distributed them. He could observe a feeling of surprise in them. The next day, it was his turn to be surprised. Mohan the senior most clerk of his depot came to his cabin and invited him to take lunch with all of them. Ram took his lunch box and went on with him to have lunch. Needless to mention, suddenly the whole atmosphere of the depot changed. Ram, who used to feel himself among strangers, suddenly found himself among friends. Since that day, everyone started listening to his suggestions.

Responsibility

Both McGregor and Herzberg emphasized the importance of responsibility as a key to motivation. Responsibility motivates a person or team towards the achievement of tasks. Assuming responsibility alone may not be enough; a team needs to have the required authority as well. Teams that have both, responsibility and authority tend to maintain their motivation for a longer period. However, taking responsibility can also be de-motivating. For example, if in past the teams were punished for making mistakes, no one will be willing to accept responsibilities in future. Therefore, in order to sustain high performance of your team members you need to create an environment free from fear, where people can come forward to accept responsibilities.

> **"When people are highly motivated, it's easy to accomplish the impossible. And when they're not, it's impossible to accomplish the easy."**
>
> **— Bob Collings**

Effectiveness of a team also depends upon how well each of its members takes up assigned areas of responsibility and designs course of action and strategies to accomplish the team's goal. You must provide them enough freedom and empowerment to feel the ownership necessary to accomplish the goal. However, members should clearly be told about their boundaries, it might be the limit for expenses or taking an important decision.

Your objective should be to make them self-reliant. You must infuse in them a feeling that they themselves can solve their problems, improve the processes, can set their goals and be able to measure the progress. Team members themselves should be able to establish norms or rules of conduct in areas such as conflict resolution, consensus decision-making, and meeting management.

George is the senior branch manager in a private bank, which has branches all over the country. Recently he got transferred to Ahmedabad from Bangalore. He was very happy when he first met his teammates. All of them were young boys and girls in their late twenties. He himself was in early thirties. He thought it would be fun working with a group of enthusiastic, young professionals. On the contrary, he found most of them timid and lacking initiative. Even for trivial issues they came to him for his opinion. Most of them seemed to be apprehensive, which was apparent from their behaviour. On provoking, directly or indirectly, they communicated the incidents, which revealed the reason for their state of mind. They were never given an opportunity to take their decisions, rather they received sarcastic comments or negative reinforcement whenever they took initiative. Some people were even punished when their decisions could not produce expected results. ▶

He called a meeting of his teammates. He started the meeting by disclosing his objective, "Friends let us make our branch the best branch in Gujarat." "How can we achieve this feat?" he asked. There was silence and then one person remarked sarcastically, "It is good to talk about becoming No. 1, but do we know what it needs to be a No. 1 branch?" George could understand the sarcasm and invited his teammates to give their viewpoints. With some hesitation people started opening up. They came out even with suggestions, which George thought of requesting them to implement. At once, the situation changed, everyone seemed interested in giving his proposition.

Seeing their interest, George asked them to write their responsibilities. Once everyone had completed, he asked them to design the course of action and strategies to accomplish their goals. He assured them the freedom to operate. He also encouraged them to find the solutions to their problems, improve the processes, and measuring the progress. He could see the transformation of his team from a dull one that lacked aggression into a team full of charge, committed to succeed.

The branch was declared the best branch not only in Gujarat but in the entire west zone.

Communication

You must ensure that team members communicate clearly and honestly with each other. Instead of spending their time pointing fingers at each other they must bring diverse opinions to the table and must resolve conflicts by themselves. This will bring the team members closer to each other. Team members will genuinely like each other and work hard to develop and maintain their relationships. It is a lot easier to support your team member when you have good relationships. This will also lead to open and direct communication among the team members, frequent praising of each other's contributions and offering mutual support.

It is not possible that all your team members will like each other. Most of the time the likes and dislikes depend on how well they understand each other. Human beings differ from each other due to their personalities, temperaments, cultures, values, beliefs, ideologies, religions, and idiosyncratic behaviours. The key to breaking these barriers is to improve the understanding among the team members. Although, most of us work in teams, majority of our interactions can be labelled as formal, serious, important, necessary, technical and administrative.

> **" A unique relationship develops among team members who enter into dialogue regularly. They develop a deep trust that cannot help but carry over to discussions. They develop a richer understanding of the uniqueness of each person's point of view."**
> **— Peter Senge**

Planning an off-site activity for the team is a powerful way of bringing team members closer to each other. It also ensures better understanding of one another. It could be a picnic, an outing or simply a celebration after a well-accomplished task, etc. You may also utilize the opportunity during the annual sport event or founder's day function, etc. These activities pull people together, provide them an opportunity to pull back, relax, celebrate what has been accomplished, and look at each other as fellow humans, bound together by a common purpose. It allows for greater interaction between people separated even by the functional boundaries. This interaction then gives them the opportunity to see their colleagues from a different perspective. This also helps them break down those hidden barriers to open communication.

I was told this incident by my friend Rohit, who was working for an MNC. In his initial days as a manager, Rohit had 7 members in his team. They used to assemble every 45 days for a review session. Rohit always took this as an opportunity to bring his team members closer to each other. In the evening after the session they used to sit together over a drink. During this time there was no boss or subordinate, everybody was equal. They used to have lots of fun. No shop talk was allowed during the evening sessions. Rather, the group penalized the person who used to initiate a business talk. This has not only brought his team members closer to each other, but also helped him in achieving his team goals. What is more, even today, after 20 years the team members are in touch with each other.

Coordination

In order to ensure that the team members work together effectively and in perfect harmony, it is important that they understand and respect the roles and responsibilities of each individual team member. Nevertheless, each and every team member must be clear about the priority of his own tasks. They should know how their performance will be measured. In addition, you must establish the method for the teams to receive honest performance feedback. You must provide important information regularly. This understanding will bring lots of seriousness in them.

In short, it is important for you to create the feeling among your team members that you are really interested in change, that you value creative thinking, unique solutions and new ideas. You must provide rewards and recognition when teams are successful. You must encourage and reward people who take reasonable risks. You must be able to provide them training, education, access to books and films, and field trips necessary to stimulate new thinking.

> **"Individuals make teams that ultimately deliver results."**
>
> **— Unknown**

You must spend time and attention to ensure your team contributes effectively to your business success. Keep in mind that individuals make teams that ultimately deliver results. Each individual team member is different in his personality and capability. Therefore, give an extrovert person the responsibilities that involve interacting with people, and assign an introvert or shy person a job that he can do alone. Your team will be full of empowered people who are on their "own" and responsible for their work processes. Your team members will love you, your business will soar, and your work life will be more rewarding.

Arvind is the branch manager of a premium insurance company. He is a smart and experienced person. He knows that different people have different styles and it is easier to capitalize on the strengths of an individual rather than fighting with them to adapt your style. Therefore, he keenly observes a person during the interview itself to recognize his potential. After joining, Arvind keeps a watch on the activities and the responses of his colleagues to different situations. This gives him an idea about the individual's working style. Accordingly, he assigns tasks to them. This is one of the reasons for his branch being the best branch of the zone. ▶

- He counts on Joseph and Reena when he has to delegate a task that is urgent and important. He found them bright and swift in their actions. They are capable of solving problems and delivering timely results.
- To Amjad and Maria he has assigned customer service and new product sales, as they possess pleasing personalities, are extroverts and have presence of mind.
- To Rajesh and Suresh, who are intelligent and methodical in their approach, he has assigned the job of streamlining the existing operating procedures and also that of developing better organizing systems.
- To Rushita and Kapil who have a knack to work on the details, he has assigned the job of analysing the competitor's policies and strategies.

POINTS TO REMEMBER

MOTIVATING A TEAM

- In a motivated team, the members work in perfect harmony to produce the desired results.
- People are often more motivated by how they are used in a job than by how they are treated. Where people feel they are part of an experiment or part of a project, they show a higher level of motivation.
- "To do it right, the first time", remains the motto of an effective team.
- Initiative breeds innovation. Taking the lead is a great risk, yet these risks are greatly reduced in a team whose members respect each other, forgive mistakes of colleagues and forego individual differences.
- In an effective team every member respects the time of others by turning team priorities into personal priorities.
- To be a part of a team is like being a part of a family, where every team member respects and values the opinions of the other members. There is mutual trust among the team members.
- It is important that each of the members should clearly understand the goal of the team. If the goal is clear to the team members and if they feel that it is in line with their own wants and needs, their motivation will be sustained, else it may diminish gradually.
- A challenge leads to a rewarding team experience. Even a mediocre team responds to a challenge with heroic success. Challenge itself works as a motivator.
- If people find their job a source of growth in their competencies, they feel motivated. This also adds value to the individual and helps them enhance their self-esteem and self-worth.
- Teams that have both the responsibility and authority tend to maintain their motivation for a longer period. In order to sustain the high performance of team members one needs to create an environment free from fear, where people can come forward and be ready to accept responsibilities.

▶

- Open and direct communication among team members, frequent praising of each other's contributions and offering mutual support develops a bond among the team members.
- Planning an off-site activity is an effective way of bringing the team members closer to each other.
- In order to ensure that the team members work together effectively and in perfect harmony it is important that they understand and respect the roles and responsibilities of each individual team member.

Synopsis

Most of us got promoted into a management or leadership role because we were good at the earlier job or task. This does not necessarily mean that we will be successful in getting the same job done from others. I am sure after reading the book you can now say with confidence, *"I can not only take a horse to the pond, but also make it drink."*

Well, the different concepts discussed in the book must have helped you sharpen your understanding about 'Motivation'. However, it is practice that makes a person perfect. Therefore, whenever confronted with the following feelings,

- "Why do I always get bad people (colleagues and superiors) to work with?"
- "Why doesn't he obey my instructions?"
- "I have never met such an ungrateful person."
- "I love my people. Why does this colleague hate me?"
- "This person just wants to embarrass me."

instead of sitting back and cursing others, you must try to recall what you learned from the book.

- Motivation is intrinsic, residing within oneself.
- Motivation is the force that causes people to act or behave differently.
- There are different reasons for different people for the same act.
- Human needs for sustenance, safety, security, belonging, recognition, sense of growth and achievement become strong drivers (motivators) of human behaviour.
- What motivates one person does not necessarily motivate another.
- Different people have different needs for motivation to grow or continue to do their job.
- A person's desire and interest decides the extent of his success. More

the desire and interest towards a particular job, better is his chance of success.

- It is the individual's motivation that propels him to do or not to do a particular act.
- A motivated individual always has a strong desire to achieve and, therefore, directs all his efforts towards the accomplishment of the goal.
- A motivated individual is dedicated to the cause and, therefore, puts in his best in whatever he does.
- When a motivated individual encounters a block, physical or mental, instead of getting frustrated, he tries to find an alternative path of reaching the goal.
- The level of motivation varies between individuals and within individuals at different times.
- People are often more motivated by how they are used in a job than by how they are treated.
- 'Motivation' is getting somebody to carry out the same task because he wants to do it, whereas it is 'Manipulation' if you expect somebody to carry out a particular task because you want him to do it.
- The performance of a team is an outcome of motivation, ability and above all the environment at workplace/home.
- In a team people think and feel differently. It is their self-confidence their beliefs in themselves, their attitude towards life, be it negative or positive. It is how they feel about their future and how they react to the past that decides their actions/behaviours.

Therefore, in order to get best out of this book you must use it as a reference point. As and when you encounter a situation that is leading to demotivation of your team members, you can dip into the related topic. Learning from this book will help you to keep people around you motivated and productive.

Wish you all the best!

Postscript

CHECK FOR YOURSELF: ARE YOU A MOTIVATED MANAGER?

In order to assess your motivation level, rate yourself on the following statements on a scale of 1 to 5.

- **5 means: strongly agree**
- **4 means: somewhat agree**
- **3 means: neither agree nor disagree**
- **2 means: somewhat disagree**
- **1 means: strongly disagree**

1. I motivate my team members to deliver their best.
2. I am making a valuable contribution to both my team as well as my organization.
3. I always set clear-cut goals for my team members and myself.
4. I always set a deadline for achieving goals.
5. I have a positive and healthy self-image.
6. I am confident and communicate assertively, both upward and downward.
7. I believe in myself and my attitude is positive.
8. I never give excuses for my failure or for my inability to perform as expected.
9. I am enthusiastic and always filled with positive feelings.
10. I lead by example.
11. I respect the time of others, hence, I remain punctual every time.
12. I know each of my team members very well.
13. I am concerned about achieving positive results from my team members.
14. I am open with my team members.

15. Quite often, I display confidence in my team members.
16. I am fair to both my team members and the company.
17. I am moving forward, learning new concepts to add to my knowledge/ skill base.
18. I stretch my mind to generate 'Out-of-the-box ideas' for problem solving.
19. I am adding value to myself and this feeling enhances my self-esteem and self-worth.
20. I allocate time for my family too, while planning my work schedule.

CHECK FOR YOURSELF: IS MY TEAM MOTIVATED?

In order to assess the motivation levels of your team, ask your team members to rate the following statements on the scale of 1 to 5

- 5 means: strongly agree
- 4 means: somewhat agree
- 3 means: neither agree nor disagree
- 2 means: somewhat disagree
- 1 means: strongly disagree

1. We are committed to accomplish our team goal.
2. We not only understand but also respect the roles and responsibilities of each individual team member.
3. Every member of our team clearly knows about the expectations of the team leader from us.
4. We are provided rewards and recognition on a well-accomplished task.
5. We are provided opportunities to upgrade our knowledge and skill base through training, education, access to books/libraries and professional courses.
6. We are provided the support needed to accomplish the set goals.
7. We are encouraged to accept a challenging task and all of us involve ourselves during group activities.
8. We are assigned responsibilities along with required authority to take appropriate decisions.
9. We are questioned but not punished for any mistakes arising out of our decisions.
10. We are provided enough freedom and empowerment to design the course of action and strategies to accomplish the team's goal.
11. We realize that taking the lead is a great risk, yet these risks are greatly reduced in our team by forgiving mistakes of one another and foregoing our individual differences.
12. While working in our team we always feel as part of the project, a family, where every team member respects/values the opinions of other members.

13. Even though each individual works in a specific department or is assigned a specific job function, all of us are unified to accomplish the overall team's objectives.
14. All of us consider ourselves as part of a team. We know that everything we do or don't do impacts our team's performance. Hence, we make sure that whosoever's job it may be it must be done.
15. In our team all of us respect the time of others by turning team priorities into personal priorities. All of us arrive for meetings on time, share information promptly, communicate concisely, and above all seek information from one another.
16. In our team people value individual suggestions, communicate openly, manage differences, share successes and welcome ideas even from a new member.
17. In our team no one points finger at another, rather we bring diverse opinions to the table and resolve conflicts among ourselves.
18. Quite often we are taken on an off-site activity such as a picnic, or simply a celebration of a well-accomplished task, etc.
19. Our team provides us an opportunity to grow and take on higher responsibilities.
20. Above all, our team provides us an opportunity to enhance our self-esteem/self-worth.

Scoring key:
Are you a motivated manager?

- A score of 81 to 100 means you are a motivated manager.
- A score of 61 to 80 means you are motivated. However, you need to push yourself a little more.
- A score of 41 to 60 means you are not putting enough efforts to remain motivated.
- A score of 20 to 40 means you are demotivated.

Scoring key:
Is my team motivated?

- A score of 81 to 100 means your team is highly motivated.
- A score of 61 to 80 means your team is motivated.
- A score of 41 to 60 means despite your efforts, your team is not feeling motivated.
- A score of 20 to 40 means your team is highly demotivated.

RELIABILITY STUDY OF THE INSTRUMENT: 'ARE YOU A MOTIVATED MANAGER?'

In order to check the dimensionality and reliability of this instrument a survey of people from across the industry was carried out. The respondents included pharmaceutical sales representatives/managers, research scientists, sales representatives/managers from the telecommunication industry, textile, information technology and customer relationship personnel from the airlines industry, etc. There were a total of **109** respondents who have attempted this instrument. While doing the factorial analysis using principal component analysis, six components emerged. Varimax rotation was carried out so that these six components could be interpreted as dimensions underlying the data. The details and interpretation of the analysis are given below.

Question numbers 1, 2, 5, 17 & 19 — **Speaks about your competency as a leader** (It is about your effectiveness in the role as a manager/leader. You believe in your role and its positive contribution towards you and your team members' development.)

Question numbers 12, 13 & 14 — **Speaks about your concern towards your team members** (It is about your relationship with your team members, wherein the basic premise is: being open and concerned leads to building an effective team.)

Question numbers 8, 10, 11, 15 & 20 — **Speaks about your leadership style** (It is about your belief that leadership can be established by setting examples and taking genuine interest in team members.)

Question numbers 6, 7 & 16 — **Speaks about how assertive you are while dealing with people** (It is about how confident you are, how much do you believe in yourself. How open and fair are you to people, how comfortable you feel while exercising your rights.)

Question numbers 3 & 4 — **Speaks about your focused approach as a manager** (It is about your understanding of the manager's role in a team, i.e. giving direction and fixing a deadline for ensuring the completion of activities.)

Average Scores of the Test Population:

Question numbers 1, 2, 5, 17 & 19:	4.12
Question numbers 12, 13 & 14:	4.21
Question numbers 8, 10, 11, 12 & 15:	3.85
Question numbers 6, 7 & 16:	4.03
Question numbers 3 & 4:	3.74

If the average score given by you is much more than the average score of the test population*, you can consider that you are a motivated manager. However, if the average scores for any of the cluster of statements given by you is less than the scores of the test population, it means you need to improve in that particular area.

This instrument will help you work on the specific areas you need to improve in order to keep yourself motivated.

RELIABILITY STUDY OF THE INSTRUMENT 'IS MY TEAM MOTIVATED?'

In order to check the dimensionality and reliability of this instrument too, a survey of people from across the industry was carried out. The respondents included, pharmaceutical sales representatives/managers, research scientists, sales representatives/managers from telecommunication industry, textile, information technology and customer relationship personnel from the airlines industry, etc. There were a total of 113 respondents who attempted this instrument. While doing the factorial analysis using Principal Component Analysis, five components emerged. Varimax rotation was carried out so that these five components could be interpreted as dimensions underlying the data. The details and interpretation of the analysis is given below.

Question numbers 1, 2, 19 & 20	**Speaks about people's loyalty/ feelings towards the team.** (It reflects the commitment of the people towards the team and their belief that working in a team is beneficial for them.)
Question numbers 4, 5 & 18	**Speaks about how much recognition is offered to them.** (It reflects people's feelings towards recognition and rewards that are offered to them.)
Question numbers 6, 12 to 17	**Speaks about importance given to team members by you.** (This talks about the cohesiveness of your team.)
Question numbers 7, 8, 9, 10, 11 & 12	**Speaks about your acceptance as a leader by them.** (It reflects upon your leadership style and their acceptance of you as their leader.)

Average Scores of the Test Population:

Question numbers 1, 2, 19 & 20:	4.37
Question numbers 4, 5 & 18:	4.54
Question numbers 6, 12 to 17:	4.45
Question numbers 7, 8, 9, 10 & 11:	4.45

You must calculate the average scores for each of the cluster separately from the responses given by your team members. If the average score given by your team members is much more than the average score of the test population, your actions are in the right direction to keep your team motivated. However, if the average score for any of the cluster of statements given by your team members is less than the average marks of the test population, it means you need to improve in that particular area. Therefore, the real benefit you will derive out of this instrument is by going into the depth of responses given by your team members for each of the clusters of statements and introspecting on your actions that might have led to your team members evaluating you and your team.

This instrument will help you increase the satisfaction levels of your team members.

**(Both the studies were conducted by Ms. Nivedita Kothiyal under the supervision of Prof. (Retd.) Pramod Verma, Indian Institute of Management, Ahmedabad.)*